REAL🔥PASSION REVOLUTION

10 **SECRET** *Ingredients for Healed, Healthy Happy Relationships*

Denise Darlene TLC

Publisher: Jesse Krieger
Write to Jesse@JesseKrieger.com if you are interested in publishing through Lifestyle Entrepreneurs Press

Publications or foreign rights acquisitions of our catalogue books.
Learn More: www.LifestyleEntrepreneursPress.com

CONTENTS

DEDICATION

I write with deep devotion to my birth children, Jonathan, Ryan, & Logan, as well as to all of my *other* children—you know who you are.

May you experience *Love*, passion, fulfillment, freedom and abundant joy with your chosen lover all the days of your lives together.

Loving You,
Momma

GRATITUDE

It is with the deepest sense of gratitude that I acknowledge those people who lovingly supported this work. Without you I couldn't have pulled this off. You made this journey possible and wonderful!

My beautiful lover, Joe, you inspired me to put all of these concepts in writing. You encouraged me to continue writing when I felt overwhelmed or discouraged— when I repeatedly tried to abort writing this book. You convinced me that I had a valuable message to share with the world, and so I am! You have been a beautiful teacher—a mirror of both my strengths as well as my weaknesses. You, Joseph Paulicivic III, are my hero, my biggest fan, my loudest cheerleader, my best friend, and my amazing lover. Thank you, my darling Joe!

Many dear friends read (and re-read) my manuscripts and gave me valuable feedback to support this work. There are those who financially contributed to getting this work published and printed as well. With gratitude and love I say "Thank You" to Jevon, Brenda, David, Danielle, Aaron, Todd, Linda, Daniele, Suzanne, [b]ecker, and Chelsea.

Lastly, and most importantly, I am beyond grateful and humbled by *Spirit* for inviting me to participate in the healing of His Beloved children. It is my sincere hope that I have presented this material in a way that honors *Love* and empowers everyone who reads this book to live their lives fully and to Love boldly.

Thank You, Papa!

Loving You,
Denise

SPONSORS

Diamond Sponsor: Joe Paulicivic

Gold Sponsors: Dave Douglass & Charla and Phil Bird

Silver Sponsor: Jevon & Carolyn Perra

Bronze Sponsors: Andie Ysais, Heather & Derick Berry, Jesse Krieger, Joey Colombo

iAM DENISE DARLENE

"I am here only to be truly helpful... I am content to be wherever He wishes, knowing He goes there with me. I will be healed as I let Him teach me to heal."

~ A Course In Miracles

I am a retired nurse, a certified Transformational Love Coach, an Author, an ordained minister, a certified Biblical Counselor, and Spiritual Teacher. I was married 33 years and have three beautiful adult sons. I worked as a nurse for five years before my second son was born, after which I was a full-time wife and mother. I have been a Transformational Love Coach since 2006. My coaching focus is all about transforming the way people *Love* themselves and others. My passion is supporting people to experience the highest quality relationships possible through an unconventional approach to healing and happiness.

I have been a student of human behavior, of God, and of *Love*, for about 38 years now. The majority of my *Spiritual* life was spent in the traditional Christian faith until 2003. While I consider myself a student of Jesus, I do not subscribe to all of the traditional doctrines taught in the Christian faith. Nor do I think that anyone has to believe what I believe to have an intimate relationship with *God*. I respect and honor everyone's *Spiritual* journey.

My Story

It wasn't long into my 33-year marriage that I became frustrated and fearful regarding the future of my relationship with my husband and our three sons. My dreams were shattered when I realized I was married to a chronic alcoholic who had been secretly drinking to manage his anxiety since the age of twelve.

After seventeen years of marriage and three children I felt stuck. From my perspective, I had two choices: to stay married and suffer the fears associated with my husband's drinking or leave and suffer the fears I had of the judgments of others and figuring out how to take care of my children and myself without a career to fall back on.

Many times I felt lonely without the companionship and fellowship of a healthy partner. I deeply loved my husband and wanted my marriage to work out. I came from a childhood of multiple failed relationships and I didn't want my children to suffer the losses I had as a child. I longed for a husband who I could lean upon who would comfort me when my own fears surfaced. Instead I felt the need to protect my husband so he wouldn't feel the stress or anxiety that typically drove him to self-medicate. I felt burdened with the responsibility of keeping our home-life running smoothly and keeping our children from experiencing the impact of a binge drinker.

My life vacillated between chaos and relief; expecting, but never really knowing when the next shoe would drop. And then it would hit and I would go into triage mode, managing the chaos and protecting my children.

It was during those challenging years I choose to learn everything I could about human behavior, emotional healing, and Spiritual enlightenment to gain the skills necessary to not only survive an unhappy marriage, but to thrive in it as well.

For sixteen more years my wounded husband became my greatest teacher. I experienced unprecedented growth in every area of my life! I became more loving, patient, compassionate, and peaceful as a result of diving into personal development. The last years were by far the most difficult for me. I now believe I simply stayed longer than the "lessons" I was there to learn. Had I followed my heart and Spirit, I would have left in peace. But, I chose to stay because I was still a slave to my fears.

Being in a relationship with a chronic addict has many challenges that others don't experience. As a result of the tools I had developed over the years, I was able to remain loving and happy for the last 16 years despite the choices my husband was making. It wasn't until the last year of my marriage, when the pain of staying became so much bigger than the fear of leaving, that I finally chose to follow my heart and my intuition into the unknown, the unfamiliar, and the possibility of something beautiful.

I am not suggesting that anyone who is struggling in their relationship should leave. On the contrary, with the exception of physical or emotional abuse, I believe that the revolutionary tools I have developed can have a significant impact for transforming a relationship from broken to beautiful, and from hurtful to happy. At the very least, these tools transformed **me** into the happy, peaceful, compassionate, loving woman I am today and have equipped me to have the romantic relationship of my dreams!

What I Believe

....

- I believe that the terms "*God*" and "*Love*" are synonymous. Therefore, I will use them interchangeably throughout this book. Anytime I refer to "*Love*," I am referencing both the concept and *God* because I believe that when we are *Loving*, we are giving expression to *God* within us. Whenever I am referring to God using a descriptive word, it will be capitalized and in italics.

- I believe that all creation is an expression of *Love* at its essence.

- I believe that *Love* is all that matters because *Love* alone endures throughout all eternity; it is the only thing we will find after our human experience.

- I believe that *Love is Energy* without form, both masculine and feminine. I prefer to relate to *God* as a male figure—particularly, as my *Papa*. I choose to relate to *Energy* this way because I never had a "father connection." I can get my need fulfilled through this personal interpretation of *Love*.

- I believe that we are all as innocent as children from *Love's* perspective. I believe the opposite of "innocent" is wounded—not guilty.

- I believe that wounded people wound others, which is where our relationship conflicts originate.

- I believe *Love* designed us to be abundantly happy!

- I believe we are all born with an ego, and that's where it all gets messy.

- I believe the ego's ultimate goal is to create the illusion that we are separate, rather than *One* with *Love* and each other. The concepts I teach are a lesson in edging the ego out and healing our *Spirit* so that we can *Love* well, rather than continually wound ourselves and others.

My Values

- My relationship with *Papa* is my deepest joy, peace, fulfillment, and purpose.

- Connecting deeply with others is both my service and my passion.

- I am committed to facilitate healing and happiness for anyone who is ready and willing to do the work to transform his/her life.

- I adore my children and am committed to maintain a loving, safe, supportive relationship with them.

- I am sensitive and compassionate towards everyone I meet without critical judgments.

- I am passionate about a life of continual evolution and empowerment, vitality, happiness, freedom, and an ever-increasing capacity for compassion and love for myself and others.

- I am *God's* Beloved. And, Dear Friend, so are you. This is why I will be referring to you as "My Friend" throughout this book. You are a precious gift of *Love* from *Love* to this world. You are *God's* Beloved and part of my family. You are my brothers and sisters, so you are precious to me as well. I want the best for you. My desire for you is that what I share with you here will facilitate your wholeness and greater happiness, which will flow into all of your relationships, especially into your most intimate relationship with your lover.

I have created a revolutionary program to heal our *Spirit*, which is our true essence. So that we can enjoy optimal relationships with everyone. So that we can be an expression of *Love* and *Joy* that compels others to want what we are experiencing. And, so that we can experience a *Real Passion Revolution* in our romantic relationships and leave a legacy of *Love* for others to follow.

THE INSPIRATION

I wanted to address the breakdown in relationships and offer the same tools that my lover, Joe, and I use every day to support a *Loving*, peaceful, safe, authentic, passionate relationship. While I am the author of this book in the traditional sense, I recognize that I am, at best, a coauthor. Everything helpful and healing was inspired by *Love* within me and by *Love* within my mentors. Joe has been a significant contributor to this work as well. For these influences in my life, I refer to this manuscript as *Our* book and *Our* work for I did not, and could not have, figured all of this out on my own.

A word about my mentors: You will read about the people who have influenced my own beliefs and changed my life for the better. I am constantly investigating beliefs: mine and others'. While I have embraced much of my mentor's teachings, I have never accepted *everything* any one person has taught. I look for what is relevant in my own life. I experiment with new and unfamiliar concepts to see what works and what doesn't for myself. My commitment to you is to only offer here what actually works for me. This relationship recipe is revolutionary and contrary to the way 99 percent of people engage with each other; if you apply these principles, they will work for you. My encouragement to you is that you stay open and curious enough to "try on" everything I'm offering in this book—like tasting something you have never tried before.

Shortly after I met Joe, I asked him if he liked rhubarb pie. Without hesitation, he said, "No!" I asked, "Have you tried rhubarb pie?" He said, "I haven't. But it sounds awful!" I laughed out loud.

I firmly believe that these concepts can have a significant impact to better your life. *Our* desire is to bring healing, happiness, and real passion back into romantic relationships through *Our* book, workshops, couples retreats, and coaching. As you are working through this book, if you feel stuck and would like to process these concepts with me as your personal coach, please visit my website where you will find both private and group coaching options.

Much Love and Devotion

Denise Darlene TLC

www.denisedarlene.com

THE VISION

My Friend, do you long to be truly known and deeply Loved? Are you tired of performing for others to feel accepted? Do you long to just be accepted for who you are, warts and all? Do you dream of a safe person to process your wounds and disappointments with, without judgments or criticism? Do you desire a partner who has the capacity to see past the messiness of your ego into your wounded Spirit?

I suspect you've been asking the *Universe* to help you find the tools to bring healing and wholeness to your relationship with your lover. You may even be asking for effective tools that will equip *you* to be the *Loving* partner *you* long to be for someone special. Do you desire a relationship where there is never an unkind word spoken? Is it possible for there to be just one person in this world who isn't critical, who isn't telling you that you're not enough that you need to change and who isn't trying to control you? Are you tired of all the bickering, resentments, frustration, lack of communication, and misunderstandings? Are you just plain tired, My Friend?

Are you lonely? Do you think you have to settle for far less than you hoped for at the beginning of your relationship? After all, don't all relationships deteriorate along the way? Why should yours be special, fulfilling, beautiful? Are you simply expecting too much?

I know that you are experiencing one or more of these longings. How do I know this about you, My Friend? Because *you* are reading *this* book. *You* attracted *this* book into your life for such a time as this! For just like you, I attracted all of my teachers when I was ready for the next step in my own *Spiritual* evolution.

You see, these were my longings too. Like you, I knew I was designed to have a beautiful, loving, supportive, passionate relationship. I knew it wasn't a fantasy that I was searching for inspired by a Disney movie. I knew this longing was a reality I could co-create given the right tools. I didn't just long for this experience, I begged *God* for it. I wanted a lover who would be my greatest fan, my loudest cheerleader, and a safe shelter in which to hide away from a judgmental world. I wanted a lover who would inspire me to grow—a man who would challenge me beyond my comfort and to empower me to live the life that *Love* purposed for me.

My own longings connected me to what is needed and wanted in every romantic relationship and revealed to *me* what *I* needed to *give* to my lover. I also knew that I would have to teach my partner how to *be* in a relationship like this since I had never seen this relationship before and I knew it was very rare indeed.

My journey on planet Earth has taught me many wonderful insights about human behavior and *Spirituality*, through personal challenges and victories, as well as from a few brilliant mentors.

- I have learned a higher purpose for romantic relationships than the crippling status quo.

- I have learned how to recognize the judgments I have of others as a mirror for self-reflection and growth.

- I have learned how the laws which govern the universe are set up and how to work effectively *with* them rather than ignorantly resist them.

- I have learned the difference between using controlling behaviors and embracing free choice in every relationship.

- I have learned about the profound impact forgiveness has on our lives.

- I have learned how to heal my emotional wounds and the impact that has on my happiness and on all of my relationships.

- I have learned about the significance and power of surrendering to *Divine* guidance within.

- I have learned about our differences through personality profiles, the different ways we give and receive *Love*, and the most significant distinctions between men and women.

- Most importantly, I have learned how to engage in an intimate relationship in a way that produces what I have longed for and prayed for all of my adult life.

Every bit of this knowledge is significant information that will support you, My Friend. But I have also learned that none of it is the key, in and of itself, to transform you or your relationship and produce a *Real Passion Revolution* in your life. It wasn't until I *combined* all of these principles together, like a recipe of sorts, that all of this knowledge became a powerful tool to create and support what I had been longing to experience.

"Write the book you want to read" was the advice I received while searching for yet another book on improving romantic relationships. What I have written here are the best concepts I have learned in the past 35 years. These are my favorite tools and principles I use to govern my own life every single day. And, the best part for you, My Friend, is that all of it is right here in one book. You don't have to filter through a library of books to find one that *might* work for you, nor do you have to read over 100 books to get the best relationship tools and content available. You only need to sit down with me and allow these words of wisdom to sink into your *Spirit* as I expound upon my personal experiences of what works and what doesn't work in relationships. For I am now experiencing the **Loving**, safe, passionate relationship I always believed was possible, and I'm writing this book so you can too.

My Friend, I am going to take you on an adventure of transformation through my own experiences, relationships, and mentors. While all of the events and experiences are real, the names and details have been changed to protect the privacy of my friends and clients.

If you are currently in a relationship, I strongly encourage you to invite your lover to join you on this journey and read this book together. I have been successfully coaching couples with these concepts by having them work through one chapter a week, taking time each evening during the week to review the content of the chapter they are working through with each other. I suggest they discuss what they are learning and share where they see they have made mistakes with each other. I encourage them to talk about how they are applying these concepts at work, with friends, and with family, and the impact they are noticing as a result of this new, unconventional approach in relating to others. I invite them to declare their new intentions with their lover.

There are many new concepts for you to implement so go slowly. One "Ingredient"/chapter per week is enough to digest and process so you can assimilate everything fully. The goal is not to finish the book quickly. The goal is to become so familiar with these concepts that they become your default way of being in relationships. If you go through this material too quickly without massaging the content into your everyday life, day after day, you will miss it. You will likely get to the end of the book with the same results as before you started reading and blame the book as useless. I promise you this: if you do the work I'm presenting here, your relationships will change radically. Even better than that, *you*, My Friend, will be transformed dramatically. You will be happy, peaceful, and content. You will be healed and on your way to being whole.

Throughout this book there will be writing exercises to help ground you in the concepts I'm teaching. You will get the most out of this material if you journal your process and answer all of the questions. Like everything else in life, you will get back what you invest so *fan the flame* with your whole heart.

I am reminded of a story of a preacher who was sent to lead a church that had recently lost its pastor. The first Sunday in the pulpit he preached a message of forgiveness and received excellent feedback from the congregation after the service. The following Sunday the pastor preached the same message for which he also received positive feedback. The next two Sundays this pastor preached the identical message. On the fourth Sunday, a member approached the pastor and said, "We all loved this message and appreciated it the first few times you preached it, but is this the only sermon you preach? Can you preach another sermon next week?" To which the pastor replied, "Sure, when you get *this* message down, I'll move onto another." Master the concepts in this book, and you will experience the most amazing transformation in your own level of happiness, freedom, and peace, as well as in all of your relationships!

Because we live in a culture of fast information at our fingertips, we have the propensity to digest information without actually *learning* it. Like the food we tend to inhale quickly, the majority of us take in much more information than we can assimilate in one sitting. Because of this cultural trend, I will repeat the concepts I'm teaching throughout this book through various stories to drill them into your awareness.

I strongly recommend you get a journal or computer diary to record your insights and process the exercises in writing. I use a computer log called *Day One*. I have formatted my daily entries in the form of a conversation with *God*. My *Day One* diary *is* my prayer time, my quiet time, my time of inquiry, of discovery, of gratitude, of listening for *God* to direct my steps according to His purpose and my best interest. In essence, my journal *is* the foundation of my personal relationship with *God*. This approach works best for me. You may prefer another method; just be sure to do the work so you can have the results that you desire.

THE CURRENT REALITY

You and I have heard story, after story, after story about failed relationships, unfulfilled relationships, and even downright miserable relationships. According to www.divorcestatistic.org, currently, the divorce rate is around 50 percent of first marriages and 60 – 73 percent of second and third marriages. Keep in mind that the *failed marriage statistics* don't include all of the *failed relationships*, which were never legally recorded. These statistics also doesn't include all of the couples who are still together but miserable. I'm sure you know many couples who fall into either or both of those camps. But aren't those *failed relationships* as well? Based on these unaccounted for relationships, I assert that the "*failed relationship statistic*" is much higher than the reported divorce statistics, which are already seriously bleak figures!

According to Attorneys.com, "When society changes, divorce changes." Three major factors over the past half century that have contributed to the current divorce rate are: 1. The "No-fault" divorce law implemented in the 1970's. Men and women no longer needed to prove abuse or infidelity to leave an unhappy marriage. 2. Woman becoming a strong force in the workplace, creating independence and financial freedom to choose to leave a miserable marriage. 3. Social acceptance. Without the guilt and shame of being divorced people are more likely to divorce. "In short, many couples that would have previously remained married now chose divorce." — *Attorneys.com*

These failed relationships are rising every decade, not because we are getting worse at marriage or relationships, rather because divorce and cohabitation are more accepted, and being happy in a relationship is the new standard. As we drop our judgments on divorce, people will have more freedom to leave a relationship that is painful and unfulfilling. However, they still won't know what *they* did to contribute to the breakdown of their relationship or how to have better results the next time around.

It's surprising that people continue to get married given these dismal statistics. I guess it's just part of our human nature—the disbelief that what happens to the majority of people will happen to us. Or, we think we are going to do "it" differently, but most of us don't! Why don't we? I believe it's because we have never taken a close look at what "it" is that *isn't working* in these committed intimate relationships.

I wanted to know why. What are we doing or not doing that is causing so much unhappiness in these close intimate relationships? How do two people start out happy and hopeful, merge their lives together, make commitments to *Love* each other for the rest of their lives, and then it all goes to hell?

Doing the same things in our intimate relationships over and over again, generation after generation, hoping for different results is insane! Obviously, something isn't working! After many years of research, personal experience, and coaching clients, I believe I have some insight to these questions.

My lover, Joe, has been my "experiment" for this material. My approach with Joe has actually changed the heart of a wounded skeptic into a rather eager, hopeful believer in a *Real Passion Revolution*, for us, and for those who join us on this journey. We hope *Our* work will bring healing to struggling relationships as well as prevent new relationships from ever experiencing the destructive effects of the status quo. *Our desire is to establish the conditions for true Love and produce a Real Passion Revolution* around the world!

The focus of this book is to support your healing, My Friend, as well as the healing of your partner. The result will be empowering, fulfilling, safe, authentic, loving, passionate relationships.

The definition of "Healing," as I am using it in this book, is to cause a shift in perspective from one of pain to power, from oppression to opportunity, from turmoil to tranquility, from victim to victor, from *fear* to *Love!* I am NOT advocating denial of any fear, pain, or anger you are experiencing. I am promoting a practice which will bring light and healing *to* your suffering. This healing, or shift in perspective, is accomplished with the guidance of your *Inner Wisdom*.

Sacred writings teach that when our thoughts are aligned with *truth*, we will experience freedom. How do we know if we believe a lie or the *truth*? By our sense of anxiety, fear, and despair or by our peace, joy, and freedom.

Chew on that for a bit and then file it away for later when I teach you how this concept works. For now, all I'm asking is that you stay open to the possibility that what I am sharing with you is true. From my own experience, there is a clear path from suffering to healing *and* freedom by understanding the application of *truth*!

The best way to get to any goal is to be very clear about where you are currently. If you want to take a trip to Florida, you need to know where you are starting the journey from. The route will be entirely different if you are starting off in Maine or California. Below is an exercise to help you get clear about your current reality, what's missing for you, and where it is exactly you want to go.

FAN THE FLAME

RELATIONSHIP ASSESSMENT:

Be specific. Example: Describe what an ideal relationship would look like for you. "I want to be able to have any conversation with my partner without him/her getting upset and shutting down." Describe what being happy looks like for you. "I would be happy if I felt confident and secure." The more time and details you give to this process, the more likely you are to achieve them.

1. What are the longings you have for an intimate relationship? (safe, passionate, compassionate, supportive, etc.)

2. What is your greatest fear regarding your intimate relationship?

3. What is the current reality of your intimate relationship? (passionate, fighting, passive, lonely, connected, distant, etc.)

4. How is this current reality impacting your life? (health, happiness, business, etc.)

5. How is this reality affecting those around you? (What are your friends and family missing out on with you as a result of your current reality? How does your relationship inspire others?)

6. As you consider these results, what are you feeling? (happy, hopeless, frustrated, content, disappointed, etc.)

7. How did you get to this place in your relationship? (Be specific. Work became more important, I was afraid to tell my partner

how I was feeling, I started nagging/complaining to feel heard and get my needs met, We made a commitment to spend quality time together, etc.)

8. If nothing changes, where do you see yourself in a year? In five years? (peaceful, stressed, content, miserable, divorced, married, etc.)

9. When these issues are resolved, and you are experiencing what you have been longing for, what difference will that make in your life? How will you feel then? (happy, fulfilled, peaceful, etc.)

10. Review your answers to question #1. Do your actions align with your desires? In other words, are you giving to your lover what you long for yourself? If not, make a list of those longings that you need to sow into your relationship. Example: If you long for a relationship where you can be authentic without any judgments, do you allow your partner to be completely authentic? Do you try to change your lover? Do you have any judgments about your partner?

It is critical that you model for your partner, or give to your lover, that which you long for, regardless of their behaviors. You must be clear about what it is you are committed to cause in your relationship in order to line up your actions with your commitment. I run all of my conversations and responses through the filter of what I am committed to have in all of my relationships—especially in my romantic relationship. I have found, without fail, that whatever has been lacking in my relationships is only what I have not given, or not given consistently in the relationship.

Stay alert and diligent, My Friend! Sow only *Love* into your relationships, and you will reap *Love* in abundance in return.

Dear God of All— In All, I believe it is You who have guided me to all of my teachers on my journey of Spiritual evolution to make me whole and full of joy. I am ready to do the work to have the results I long for in both my personal healing and for a Real Passion Revolution with my lover. Open my eyes to see what I have been blind to see until now.

And so it is, My Friend, and so it is!

Recipe Part 1

THE MAIN INGREDIENT: PURPOSE

Every recipe has a main ingredient—a foundation upon which we add other ingredients to make something delicious to eat. The other ingredients add flavor to enhance and transform the main ingredient from something bland into something that makes our taste buds dance. However, without the main ingredient, the other ingredients would be pointless. In relationships, the main ingredient or foundation is its *purpose*. The *purpose* directs every other thing we do, so the *purpose* of our relationships is significant. If our *purpose* isn't pure, it doesn't matter what we add to the relationship; it won't turn out well—like putting salt on a spoiled piece of meat.

SECRET INGREDIENT 1

THE PURPOSE OF *LOVE*

"I've told you these things for a purpose: that My joy might be your joy, and your joy wholly mature. This is My command: **Love** *one another the way I* **Loved** *you. This is the very best way to* **Love**.*"*
John 15:11MSG

I believe the main problems with every struggling relationship is first a faulty foundation (*purpose*) as well as a lack of critical tools (knowledge). Since the majority of relationships are struggling, I assert they are established upon a faulty *purpose* first and foremost. Did it ever occur to you to consider what the *purpose* of your romantic relationship should be? Not only didn't it occur to me to consider that question, but I never heard anyone else talk about the *purpose* of their relationship either.

In this section, I will point out what I believe is the *faulty purpose* of relationships that don't work (a default behavior) and contrast that with what I believe is a pure *purpose*, which does work.

First, I think it's a good idea to start with *your* reality, My Friend. I don't want just to give you information or advice; I want you to have a personal experience with these concepts to see for yourself where you want to make some changes. Besides, we all know that most of us don't listen to the advice of others. Because, even if that guidance is perfect, it just remains someone else's truth that we can dismiss or minimize by saying, "That may be true for him/her, but he/she doesn't know *my* situation." Unless it becomes *real* for us through an experience, it remains an impotent theory rather than a powerful truth or reality. I have found that by doing exercises that support a new concept, I am then able to take away what is right for me and leave behind whatever doesn't apply to *me* or what I'm not ready to receive. I invite you to do the same with this material, Dear One.

It will support you best if you **write down** your answers before reading further. I have discovered that I usually have a vague concept of answers to questions in my mind, but I can get very clear about what is going on when I write my answers down or process them out loud with someone.

FAN THE FLAME

PURPOSE EXERCISE:

1. What are the top 3 attributes which attracted you to your lover?

    a. *Ex: He is a hard worker/She is compassionate with everyone/He is super playful/She is very peaceful*

2. Now, based on the answers to the first question, which needs are being met for you with this person? *Ex:*

    a. *He is a hard worker, and that makes me feel secure; therefore, the need being met for me is security.*

    b. *She is compassionate with me, which makes me feel nurtured; therefore, the need being met for me is nurturing.*

    c. *He is super playful, which gives me a break from my seriousness; therefore, the need being met for me is fun.*

    d. *She is very peaceful, which calms my anxiety; therefore, the need being met for me is a sense of peace.*

3. As a result of what you are now aware of from answering questions 1 and 2, what do you believe is the *purpose* of your relationship?

Example:

In my relationship with Joe, besides the fact that this man is gorgeous and has the most captivating eyes, I was very attracted to his confidence, creativity, compassion, Spirituality, spontaneity, and commitment to having fun. He was attracted to my Spirituality, peacefulness, flexibility, and willingness to go along with his plans. If this were a need-based relationship, the needs being met for Joe would be peace, Spiritual growth, nurturing, acceptance, and fun. The needs being met for me would be peace, fun, security, Spiritual fellowship, and freedom.

WHAT DOESN'T WORK: A FAULTY FOUNDATION

Most people believe the *purpose* of these special relationships is to *get their* needs met; to complete themselves: "You bring your strengths that I don't have to the relationship, and I will bring mine." In the beginning, that exchange makes us happy. "I will trade you the security of your hard work in exchange for my peacefulness." From this perspective, it would be more accurate to say, "I trade you very much," rather than, "I love you very much." This exchange of strengths is where we *think* our sense of completeness and happiness. But *real* and lasting happiness is never the result of something outside of us. Read that again, Dear Friend!

Now, I ask you, My Friend, is it more empowering to *learn* what it takes to become a more peaceful person or to rely upon your lover to calm you down? Is it more powerful to discipline yourself to include fun activities in your life or depend on your lover to *drag* you out of your comfort zone to play? In most of these relationships, we don't want to change or grow ourselves; we only want our lover to do for us what we are unwilling to do for ourselves. The purpose of *this* relationship, therefore, is to "get" something.

The biggest problem with this foundation of *getting* is that it isn't limited to *getting* that one need met (the one or three or ten you were attracted to when you chose this person to be your mate); it's a whole mindset. It's the idea that your lover is supposed to *make you happy* by conforming into an image you hold of what a lifepartner does and doesn't do for you, or with you, or to you. I assert that depending on someone else to *give* you what you lack is not a good foundation on which to build a quality intimate relationship. This perspective leads to conflict down the line because no one wants to be controlled or molded into some ideal fantasy image. We want to be authentic! We long to be free—to simply *be*. When someone shows up in a way we don't like or doesn't fit *our needs and wants*, we complain, blame, nag, withdraw, and criticize in an attempt to control our lover. Any relationship based on *getting* uses strategies designed to control his/her partner into behaviors which he/she *think* will make them happy or more comfortable. In reality, those controlling behaviors undermine the relationship and lead to "irreconcilable differences."

Have you or your partner used any of those strategies to *get* something to change in your lover? No one likes that by the way!

Example:

Janet and Jim were clients of mine who were in a serious breakdown in their relationship. After a small amount of questioning on my part, I realized where the main issue was. Like all couples, these two were attracted to each other to fill a need. In the beginning of the relationship, Janet felt insecure about being able to provide for herself after recovering from a serious illness. Jim wanted to "take care" of a woman, and Janet was a "damsel in distress;" Jim felt confident he could rescue her. The problem with a dependent-codependent relationship is that if just one of the people in the relationship becomes healthier, and the other partner doesn't, there becomes a breach in the "relationship agreement." Dependents believe they are helpless to take care of themselves. Codependents need to be in a place of power in the relationship; if someone "needs" you, you're in power!

After being married a few years, Janet had become financially secure and no longer dependent upon Jim to provide for her. As a result, she began to notice Jim's controlling behaviors and she began resisting his power. Jim attached his value to his ability to "take care" of his wife. Janet was acting too independently for Jim to get his need for power and value met, so he began resisting Janet's new independence with even more controlling behaviors. Janet never saw Jim's controlling behaviors before because her neediness blinded her to all the ways Jim was unhealthy. Janet was only *looking* for someone to save her. Jim was *looking* for someone to rescue and who would submit to his control.

In this particular relationship, it appeared these two people were only compatible in the roles of "dependent/codependent;" nothing else fit. If they had other areas of compatibility and if Jim would have done some healing work of his own and released his need to control, the relationship could have been saved. Unfortunately, Jim didn't do the work, so he is bound to attract the same situation again; Janet won't. Janet did the work of healing her insecurity/dependent mindsets.

Now that you understand that *getting* a need met is the faulty foundation that most relationships are built upon, let's take a look at your answers to the questions I had you consider to make my point clearer.

Example:

If I feel insecure about being able to provide for myself, I will subconsciously be attracted to a man whom I perceive as a "hard worker," either with a secure level of success or at least the perceived potential for success. In the beginning, I may often tell him how wonderful he is for being such a hard worker; I might even brag to my friends about how responsible he is and how safe I feel with him. However, as time goes on, his work hours begin to wear on me as I find myself spending so much time alone or without his support with the house or with our kids. My partner's attractive trait worked perfectly for me at the beginning of our relationship until his work hours interfered with *my need* to spend time with him.

Guess what my strategy will be to *get* my partners attention if simply asking for more time/help doesn't work? I will complain, blame, nag, withdraw, and criticize. Guess what that will produce? Resentment, resistance, withdrawal; my partner will likely spend even more time at the office. What we resist persists! I see problems frequently arise when a partner fails to meet a perceived expectation to "*meet my needs.*" It's a crazy, predictable phenomenon that occurs with stunning regularity somewhere shortly after the relationship moves into a deeper level of commitment such as marriage or moving in together.

Getting our needs met by another person is *not* what we need to be happy. For to be happy *is* to be *healed*, My Friend. That is a powerful concept, so read it again, My Friend!

Let me remind you again of my definition of what it means to be *healed*. The definition of *healing* as I am using it in this book is to cause a shift in *perspective* from one of pain to power, from oppression to opportunity, from turmoil to tranquility, from victim to victor, from *fear* to *love!*

Having said that, when have you ever heard anyone say that their romantic relationship is *healing* for them? Have you, or anyone you know, said *anything* in their vows of their commitment to their lover about being an instrument of *healing* for their partner or a safe place to grow? I have been to many commitment ceremonies; most of the vows exchanged are similar. They speak of *Love* and *respect* in good times and bad. And yet, what we see happening over and over again, is an attempt to control their lovers to conform into an image that *they* prefer so *they* can feel good.

Pause here for a moment and consider this question: On a scale of 1 – 10, how sensitive are you? How easily are your feelings hurt when someone is critical of you? If someone is critical of you, how do you typically respond? Do you get angry? Do you defend yourself? Do you cry? Do you shut down or go silent? Do you walk out of the room? Do you feel unknown, unloved, misunderstood? Does someone's criticism of you make you want to draw closer or withdraw from the relationship? If you use criticism in your romantic relationship in an attempt to control your lover, do you think he/she feels the way you do when you are criticized?

It seems to me that we are committed to being right and clinging to our own comfort! Without hesitation, we will mow over our partner's tender heart with criticism and complaints or punishing behaviors (like withdrawal or the "silent treatment") without even the slightest awareness of the wounds we ignorantly inflict on them—all in the name of "love!" Is this what we call *Love and respect*, which we spoke of in our vows? Of course not! But, we are so desperate to *get* these perceived needs met, we are completely unconscious of our impact. When your lover criticizes, complains, or punishes you, you are clearly aware of their impact, right? If we continue to communicate to our lovers that they aren't enough, we will unconsciously undermine our relationship and their self-esteem with *our* criticism. We will ignorantly support the unwanted, unhealthy behaviors we are trying to change.

This strategy is lose-lose; nobody wins! This approach doesn't work, and yet we continue to engage in these behaviors over and over again, hoping someday we will finally *get* the desired results. Why do we continue with this insanity hoping for different results when it clearly doesn't work? Because, My Friend, we don't know what else to do! We have never been taught an alternative way of getting our needs met!

WHAT DOES WORK: A SOLID FOUNDATION OF *LOVE*

I believe these special intimate relationships are designed to be *the one place* where healing is facilitated by nurturing, encouraging, empowering, supportive *Love*, where not one critical, cynical, blaming, angry, manipulative, punishing, threatening, nagging, controlling word is spoken. This intimate relationship is the one space we get to process our wounds and messes in total safety. In *this* relationship, the ego is ignored, and the *Spirit* is affirmed. Should either partner have an off day and show up with their ego raging, *nothing* is taken personally. There is a space created in this relationship where neither partner has to be perfect. *This* is the relationship where compassion and grace abound.

The *purpose* of this relationship is to *heal* both yourself and your lover. The *purpose* of this relationship is to grow, encourage, empower, and to *give*. The *purpose* of this relationship *is Love*! *Love* asks for nothing in return, because *Love* lacks nothing! *Love* is **not** an emotion. Joy is an emotion. Joy is the *fruit* of *Love*. Joy is the *feeling* we experience when we are being *Loved* by someone or when we are *Loving* ourselves or another. *Love* is a *behavior* in the best interest of all.

I assert that *true Love* is always in the best interest of everyone regardless if it is *Love* of self or others. There is no such thing as "selfish love!" There is selfishness, but true *Love* is, by nature, other-ness! If we truly *Love* ourselves (and we absolutely should *Love* ourselves), that *Loving* behavior will also be in the best interest of others, whether they like our choices or not.

Example:

After only a few dates with Joe, it was evident to me that this precious man had been beaten down a bit by life. He was living with the subconscious belief that he *wasn't enough*. Joe's former wife had communicated to him that he was selfish (aka, he didn't do what she wanted him to do when she wanted him to do it). Joe was thoughtful enough to warn me of his "selfishness" early in our relationship; I didn't see it at all! I spent the following year reminding him that he was [is] generous, thoughtful, kind, *Loving*, and giving. Anytime Joe would reference his "selfishness," I would simply point out all the *Loving* choices he made with me, with his daughters, with his parents, with his sisters, with his nieces and nephews, and with his friends. Not only did I repeatedly interrupt the, "I'm selfish" conversation he was having with himself, I also provided as much evidence as I could to disprove that internal dialog. We are all selfish at some level. However, which do you think would facilitate fewer selfish behaviors, telling someone they are selfish, or affirming all of the unselfish choices they make?

By affirming Joe's *Loving*, kind, and generous choices, he began to drop the false belief that he was selfish and began doing *more* of what I was telling him about my experience of him. Our behaviors come from both our conscious and subconscious beliefs we hold about the world and about ourselves. This is why it is so crucial to only speak kind words to our lovers. Sacred text asserts, "As a man thinks, so is he." Henry Ford said, "whether you think you can or think you can't—you're right." If I tell you over and over again that you are selfish (because you aren't doing what I want you to do) and you believe me, then you are going to continue to act selfishly. If we are going to bring out the best in our lovers, we must be a constant source of affirmation, highlighting our lover's strengths and simply ignoring any behavior we don't want to continue.

I imagine that some of you might be feeling discouraged or a bit of despair at the thought of not being able to control some of your lover's unwanted behaviors. Or perhaps you are feeling powerless to get your lover to do something you feel you need in the relationship. Trust me when I tell you that the concepts I am teaching here will produce even more of what it is you long for. It is your controlling behaviors that are producing more of what you don't want. I will teach you how to negotiate a compromise in a *Loving* way which supports your relationship rather than causing injury in Secret Ingredient 6.

Remember, in the "Current Reality" section, at the end of the "Relationship Assessment," I encouraged you to be clear about what it is you are committed to cause in your relationship by modeling for your partner that which you long for yourself?

I have a clear intention regarding my relationship with Joe. I am committed to NEVER hurting Joe or harming our relationship, by ONLY engaging in *Loving*, supportive, affirming behaviors and conversations. I run all of my choices and conversations through the filter of: "Is what I'm about to say or do going to support or harm Joe and/or our relationship?" I am committed to interrupting any negative false beliefs Joe may have by empowering him with truth, so we can both experience his beautiful *Spiritual* potential. If Joe becomes aware of something he doesn't like in himself, he can share that with me and I will support him to change with affirmations and encouragement towards his desired goal.

My commitment to these expressions of *Love* and my strategy to empower Joe *is* the reason Joe and I are enjoying such a beautiful relationship today. It is *Love* that changed Joe's heart from fear to *Love*. *Love* begets *Love*, but only 100 percent of the time! If we *think* we have been acting in a loving way with our partner, but the fruit of the relationship is other than *Love*, we must investigate *our own* actions first. There have been many times in my relationships where I *thought* I was being loving, but the results or feedback was anything but loving.

I will expound more about this and the beautiful gift of feedback in Secret Ingredient 6.

Sacred scriptures admonish us to train our thoughts in a specific way: "… *filling your minds and meditating on things true, noble, reputable, authentic, compelling, gracious - the best, not the worst; the beautiful, not the ugly; things to praise, not things to curse." Philippians 4:8 MSG*

My Friend, if you desire a beautiful relationship, then rip up the current foundation of *getting* and establish a new foundation of *Love* by learning to *give* that which you desire to experience, that which is in the best interest of your lover. If you are now aware of some mistakes you have made with your lover through reading this first chapter, I suggest the first way to establish a new foundation is a confession of your mistakes. Let your lover know of every way you now see that you have hurt them or damaged your relationship with your words and actions. Ask your lover to share with you if you have hurt them in any other ways that you didn't mention. Then, thank them for their honesty and acknowledge their pain by asking for their forgiveness over each offense. DO NOT, DO NOT, DO NOT become defensive about anything your lover perceived as hurtful that you see differently. Only acknowledge *their* experience and move on.

Don't say, "I'm sorry." There is a huge distinction between being sorry and asking for forgiveness. Asking for forgiveness puts the ball in *their* court and allows *them* to choose to forgive you or not, if they are ready, or not. It's OK if they aren't ready to forgive you. The act of forgiving isn't about you or even *for* you; it's about *them*. Tell your lover it was never your intention to hurt them; you just didn't know then what you know now. Let your partner know what you are learning here and share with them the specific ways you intend to do things differently. Ask your lover to help you with your new commitment by letting you know if you fall back into your old, unsupportive strategies (i.e., controlling behaviors).

Do this work, My Friend, and you will experience the change you long for with your lover. *Love* will not return void!

*SECRET INGREDIENT 1 CONCEPT: *The Main Purpose of Relationships*

1. Healing for both partners
2. To establish a safe space to grow at your own rate
3. To celebrate and encourage your partner's *Spirit*
4. To give that which you long for yourself
5. Relationship Assessment

FAN THE FLAME

1. Which needs have you tried to get your lover to meet?

2. How have you tried to get your needs met in this relationship? (requesting, complaining, blaming, nagging, negotiating, threatening, punishing, rewarding, crying, acts of anger, passive-aggressive strategies, criticizing, etc.)

3. What mistakes do you now recognize you have made with your lover that have damaged your relationship?

4. Did you ask your lover to forgive you for hurting them? How did your lover respond?

5. State a new purpose for your romantic relationship.

6. What are you committed to cause (have happen) in your romantic relationship?

7. In what ways can you better support and encourage wholeness in your lover?

8. What do you long for in your relationship with your partner? What do *you* need to *give* in order to support the experience you most desire?

Dear God of All— In All, please establish Your purpose for joy in my life through the healing gift of my Beloved partner. Awaken my spirit and open my eyes to see my wounds, my stories, and my fears—my weaknesses as well as my strengths through this intimate relationship.

And so it is, My Friend, and so it is!

SECRET INGREDIENT 2

THE PURPOSE OF ATTRACTION

"Why do you look at the [insignificant] speck that is in your brother's eye, but do not notice and acknowledge the [egregious] log that is in your own eye? Or how can you say to your brother, 'Let me get the speck out of your eye,' when there is a log in your own eye? You hypocrite (play-actor, pretender), first get the log out of your own eye, and then you will see clearly to take the speck out of your brother's eye."
Matthew 7:3-5 AMP

At the beginning of my relationship with Joe, I told him, "Honey, you will *never* be my problem; you will always, and only, be my opportunity to address that which needs to be healed within me." After a long pause of shock and disbelief on Joe's face, that statement set us both free! Joe and I know that *my* problems are *not* with him, he is merely the *gift* in the moment for *me* to become aware of what requires attention on *my* part; to offer *my* wounds to *Spirit* within me for truth, healing, and freedom.

Believe me when I tell you that there have been *many, many* moments in my relationship with Joe for *me* to address *my* wounds. I am astounded at how very *perfect* this man is for me—as if he were tailor-made for my specific emotional *buttons.* Again and again, I am reminded that I have attracted this man because I require *his* specific behaviors to trigger *my* wounds so that I can be healed and set free to make choices from a place of *Love* rather than fear.

It appears that we are programmed to be attracted to our equals in life—people who are equally (although uniquely) emotionally and *Spiritually* wounded or healed. Included in this field of attraction is our subconscious drive to work through the issues we struggled with the most in our childhood, which, for many of us, was with one or both of our parents. We actually recreate the environment we experienced as children with the partner we choose as adults. Even if we are aware of this automatic attraction, and we do our best to avoid getting into a relationship with people who *further* the same childhood issues, somehow we end up with them—unless, of course, we have done the work of healing the wounds inflicted by others, and have released them. I call those wounds our *story.*

Example:

My mother shared with me that she tried to abort me by drinking turpentine when she found out she was pregnant with me. My dear mother had already been divorced, had buried her first-born child, had two other children in diapers, and was in a difficult marriage when she found out she was pregnant *again!* I was partially born with my umbilical cord wrapped around my throat in the driveway of the hospital while my father was screaming at my mother to keep her legs closed so I didn't ruin his brand new car seat. By the time the nurses got to me, I was blue from a lack of oxygen. As I was being strangled, and my mother was being screamed at during my birth process, I'm pretty sure my experience was violent and unsafe, to say the least.

I grew up in an unstable family. My father left when I was six years old, and I only saw him a few times until the age of eighteen. After my father left, my mother had to figure out how to take care of her children alone, so she went to work. I don't remember my mother being around much. My mother had a high need for belonging, but she didn't have a good "partner-picker," so she was in many relationships during my childhood, which also occupied a lot of her time and energy. As we got a little older, my oldest brother, Loren, and I were left alone much of the time. My brother was an angry youth as he was dealing as best he could with his abandonment pain. More times than I can count, Loren took his anger out on me. My mother didn't want to hear about the fighting and said I probably deserved it.

The first *story* I developed as a result of these events was, "I don't matter." I remember hoping that each of the men my mom got involved with would want to be my daddy. They didn't, which confirmed my *story*, "I don't matter."

The other dominant *story* I suffered from most of my life was, "Everybody leaves me." This *story* was the result of my interpretation of several events. First, my father left. Then, immediately after my father left, my seven-year-old brother, Brian, was placed in foster care due to a malignant brain tumor. Brian required a lot of time and financial medical care. My mother needed assistance from the state with Brian's medical expenses. She couldn't give him the care he required and take care of Loren and me, as well as try to figure out how she was going to support our little family. I imagine it scared the hell out of her to have to watch another son die a painful death since she had already witnessed her first born die at the young age of two. I was far too young to understand all of the considerations that went into the decisions my mother needed to make for all of us. I simply had the harsh facts of my reality to interpret—as a six-year-old.

Shortly after Brian was placed in foster care, my mother sent Loren and me across the country to live with my grandparents while she figured out how she was going to provide for her children. In a matter of months, I had lost my father, my brother, my mother, and my home. As you can imagine, from a six-year-old's perspective, I came to the conclusion that *everybody leaves!* My mother recounted a story from this period of my life. She said she had done my laundry, and when she went to put my clean clothes away, she discovered that my drawers were all empty. When she asked me where I put my clothes, without any emotion, very matter-of-factly, I responded, "Daddy went away, Brian went away, and when you go away I need to be ready to go somewhere too, so I'm all packed." That's the way a six-year-old connects the dots: "Everybody leaves!"

All of the men who came and left our home over the years had a profound impact on my abandonment issues. When I was in high school, my mother attempted suicide. I remember being so angry and yelling at her in the hospital, "Who's going to take care of Loren and me when you're dead?" Lastly, I watched Brian and my father breathe their last breaths as they were disconnected from life support. As you can imagine, my *stories* were confirmed and supported through my interpretations of these events.

At the age of twenty, I married my high school sweetheart, Tim. This man loved me deeply. What attracted me to him was his devotion to me. Tim made me feel like I was his world, and I was confident he would never leave me. I was also very attracted to his strong character of being a hard worker, which provided a sense of security for me that

I never had as a child. Shortly after we wed, Tim got busy working hard for our family; sounds lovely, right? The problem was Tim was both a perfectionist and workaholic. So, once we were married, he was rarely around, which made him unavailable to me emotionally *and* physically. I felt alone and abandoned again! My *story* that, "I don't matter" was supported in my relationship with my husband.

Listen carefully, My Friend, to this part. Had I understood then what I know now, I *could* have just as easily *interpreted* my husband's long work hours in a supportive way. Such as, "My husband works so hard because I matter so much to him, and he wants to provide the very best for me," which *was* true for him. However, because I had this *story* that I needed to be right about, my default, or automatic, *interpretation* was, "Tim's not around because I don't matter."

Many years later, Tim became an alcoholic, a very kind, guilt-ridden alcoholic. His alcohol abuse was so severe it threatened his life on numerous occasions. While Tim would never have left me by walking out of our marriage, when these episodes would occur, I was suddenly and painfully aware that he might die from *his choices*. As you can imagine, that supported my *story* that, "Everybody leaves me." I suffered the same pain with my husband that was initiated by my childhood experiences—abandonment and chaos! It took many years for me to make these connections and understand that Tim's choices, and mine, were recreating my childhood experiences.

You see, Darling, our *story* becomes like a radio signal searching out a particular frequency. Not only does it *always* find what it's tuned into, but it also *can't* pick up any other signal being broadcast that doesn't match the same frequency of our *story*. Nor can it receive any message that contradicts our *story*. If my *story* is, "I don't matter," then I can't receive any messages that would tell me that *I do matter*. If my *story* is,

"Everybody leaves me," then I will attract and be attracted to people who don't value relationships. Or, I will create a situation to push them away.

My subconscious strategy was to befriend people who *needed* me. If I made myself a significant value in the life of a *needy* person that would solve both problems: *I would matter,* and I would lessen the risk of them leaving me. This is also known as being a codependent. Codependents are a magnet for dependents. I captured many dependents over and over again, trying to keep people from leaving me. However, because we entered into an unhealthy relationship, I eventually became weary of bearing the responsibilities of needy people, which weren't mine to carry. When I stopped being codependent, my friends went looking for another codependent so they could continue to get their needs met. I *felt* abandoned, again and again, cementing my *stories* deep in my psyche.

Are you beginning to understand, My Friend?

Currently, I am in a relationship with Joe, who, at the beginning of our relationship, made it clear that he never wants to be married again. Joe told me that had he followed his *Intuition* in his twenties he would never have married his first wife, not because he didn't love her, rather, because he wanted to be able to keep his options open should the relationship take a turn for the worst. We recently learned that, according to an ancient *Spiritual* personality profile called, The Enneagram, Joe innately has a high need for freedom, adventure, and flexibility. Uh-oh? Is this a red-flag?

By now you might be thinking, "This woman is nuts getting into a relationship with a man who doesn't ever want to be married again." Trust me, My Friend, I am trained to *listen* to all the verbal and non-verbal cues as a relationship coach. But, let me ask you this question: Which is more powerful, to heal my childhood wounds *through* a relationship, or avoid that fear and try to find someone who said he would *never* leave me. Is it even possible to be guaranteed that someone will never leave? The answer is, "No!"

While it's true that I might *feel* less secure without a ring on my finger, I absolutely do not believe that getting married makes a relationship any more secure than entering into a commitment without making it legal. I went into this relationship with my eyes wide open with clear intentions. I wanted to face my fears, reframe my past, heal my wounds, and be a healer for Joe's beautiful *Spirit*. I have learned so much more about my fears, the lies I have told myself most of my life about relationships and events, and about healing than I could have learned without risking this adventure. By nature, all adventures worth experiencing have an element of risk, of stepping into the unknown, the unfamiliar, even facing our fears; life would simply be boring without them in my opinion.

Dear Friend, we can only take others as far as we have gone ourselves. If I am going to be healed be a healer for my lover and for the world, then I need to go first. I must go all the way to being whole and fully healed to understand what is needed and wanted, not only for my healing, but the healing of others as well.

Joe *Loves* me very much, and he is deeply committed to me. Joe's *Love* has healed me in ways I could have never imagined. He has told me many times that he loves our life together and frequently talks about our future together far into our later years. He just doesn't believe that marriage works out for most people so, why bind oneself legally to another when it's just going to end—that's his *story*! Joe recently thanked me for my commitment to our relationship in spite of his resistance (aka "fears"). I couldn't be happier or more confident with my decision.

Want a good laugh? Joe has been a wedding photographer the past 24 years. He has made a career out of photographing the day a couple enters into a legal commitment of marriage— a commitment of which he is now a skeptic since his failed marriage! Oh, and I am a Transformational *Love* Coach with a commitment to help others design passionate *Loving* relationships that are deeply fulfilling *throughout* the couple's lifetime. However, I'm in a relationship with a man who doesn't believe relationships can last! How ironic is that? Sounds like a perfect setup to test out my relationship strategies, wouldn't you agree?

I have chosen Joe because I refuse to be governed by my fears. Facing my fears head on was my first step toward wholeness! What I realize now is that if Joe ever does leave me, it won't be because *I don't matter* and it won't be because *everybody leaves me*; it will be because he requires a different gift to further his healing and growth. There is nothing *wrong* with me.

I believe Joe is perfect for me in every way as my healer, both in nurturing my wounds and exposing them. And I am equally his healer. I attracted this man into my life because I *require* him for my healing and wholeness; he pushes my biggest buttons! I also believe that Joe attracted me so he could address his fears, heal his *stories,* and have the relationship he truly desires. Does this make sense, My Friend?

Both Joe's perspective (*story)* and mine are survival strategies designed to prepare us for the disappointment of a loss. We default to listening for the warning signs or red flags that the inevitable is coming. The problem with these strategies is that we can, and do, misinterpret the words, tones, or intentions of other people in such a way that supports our personal beliefs/*stories* and we totally miss out on all the other supportive *Loving* messages those people are trying to send to us.

Like amateur attorneys, we spend our lives gathering the evidence we need to confirm our *stories*. The insane reality is, *we* recreate those *stories* over and over by our selective interpretations of events, as well as by our choices, driven by our subconscious need to be right. That means that you can change partners a million times, and you will end up with the same man or woman regardless of how careful you are about who you *think* you're choosing. You do not need a new partner, My Friend; you need to embrace the gift you have attracted and get busy healing yourself.

What I have learned about my *story* is that my deepest fear is not that everybody leaves me, rather that, *I will be alone.* Once I connected those dots, I was able to see how ridiculous that fear is. Joe has been a tremendous support in helping me to see that I am a wonderful partner, companion, *Love* coach, writer, friend, and lover, so I need not fear being alone—EVER!

Now, whenever I hear him say things that land on my *everybody leaves me* button, I simply remind myself that no matter what happens in my future, with or without him, not only will I be *Loved*, I will also be happy because my happiness lies within me, not in my circumstances.

The point I'm driving home with you, is that you and I *will* attract, and be attracted to, our wounded equal, and this, Dear Friend, is excellent news! For these *special* relationships hold within them our healing *if* we are aware of their purpose, *and* we have the tools to do the work of healing ourselves.

I hope by now you are nodding in agreement as you are putting the pieces together about your *story*.

My Friend, we don't need to be right about our *stories*! We need to be healed!

"Mirror, mirror on the wall…I'm not like him/her at all!"

If you are like most people reading this book, you're having some trouble in your intimate relationship, or you're ready to bolt and just *happened* to have picked up this book as a last resort. Now, you're probably thinking, "But, I'm nothing like him/her!" Before you throw this book at your partner, I invite you to do the Mirror Exercise in this chapter.

Not only are the partners we have attracted into our lives a *gift* to expose and heal our childhood wounds, but they are also perfect reflections of ourselves—both our strengths and weaknesses. They are an opportunity for us to take a look at what's working and not working *in our own lives* that we would not otherwise notice.

Has it ever occurred to you that your partner is a perfect resource for addressing all of your issues (those you are aware of and those you are clueless about)? At some level, all of us are conceited; we think more highly of ourselves than we are. Conceit divides us and gives us permission to judge others. This egotistical tendency is very damaging to any relationship, but especially to our romantic relationships. I have found that the best way to see oneself clearly is to take a look at our partner; *they* are our mirror, and *that* is the truth.

Example:

I coached a woman, Rhonda, who was constantly worried about her husband, Larry, because of his health issues. Rhonda did everything she could (complained, nagged, criticized, argued) to transfer her fears to Larry to get him to change his eating and drinking habits. Larry had many health issues including diabetes, obesity, high cholesterol, and high blood pressure, placing him at high risk of having a stroke or dying. Rhonda, mind you, had a few bad habits of her own. She loved sweets, was overweight, and used alcohol to quiet her fears. Rhonda didn't consider her poor choices a health risk because she hadn't been diagnosed with any diseases (yet). Had Rhonda used this tool to consider Larry as a *gift* of self-reflection, she would have seen her own poor choices and the work at hand for herself. It was not Rhonda's business to correct her husband. It *was* her business to make better choices for herself. The chances were much better that Larry would have made some changes for his own health as he saw his wife taking better care of herself. Certainly, trying to control the situation through worry and nagging didn't help one bit. That behavior did, however, trigger Larry to rebel and do more of things that bothered Rhonda.

Turns out, this relationship created a similar childhood environment for both Rhonda and Larry. As far back as Rhonda could remember, she felt responsible for her mother's health. And, Larry's mother was overly controlling. This is what we do, My Friend. We recreate our childhood environments so we can heal the wounds inflicted upon us as children.

Sacred writings tell us that when we know the truth, we will experience freedom. I assert that freedom and healing are synonymous! Healing and freedom are not what you *think* about the work you have done; it's the results that are standing right in front of you, staring you in the face, driving you up a wall; *that* is the truth!

At this point, you are likely to judge what I'm saying as good news or bad news. I strongly recommend you don't judge it; rather, embrace it and get to work!

Remember, my invitation at the beginning of this book? I told you that I would be leading you to a new paradigm of *Love* that is completely contrary to what you've always done; well, here we go, My Friend!

FAN THE FLAME

Take a good look at your partner and write down everything you would like to change about your him/her and the judgments you hold of him/her; this is the first step in your healing process.

This exercise won't work if you don't write it down, My Friend. Leave nothing out! Do not edit! You are NOT going to show this list to anyone, so be vividly honest; write down the strengths and weaknesses you see in your partner. This is not you being mean or unkind or critical; this is you being honest with what is already true for you. Do you think for one moment that your partner doesn't sense these judgments you hold? Wouldn't it be better if you were able to get these judgments out of your relationship?

Each of our judgments projects a specific vibrational energy which is transmitted to those around us. We already know what people think about us; we just aren't conscious enough to confront those judgments. You know your partner's judgments, and he/she knows yours, if not on a conscious level then certainly on a subconscious level. Our judgments *shape* our relationships because our behaviors toward our partner match our judgments. If I think my partner is an idiot, I'm not going to treat him like he's brilliant. I won't trust him or consult him on matters of significance.

Here are a few judgment adjectives to get you started:

Selfish	Prideful
Kind	Angry
Peaceful	Lazy
Controlling	Thoughtful
Irresponsible	Sensitive
Greedy	

(*You will likely have others or different judgments than the examples I have given*)

MIRROR EXERCISE 1 - JUDGMENTS

1. Take a blank sheet of paper and dump all (and I mean ALL) of the judgments you hold about your partner. Begin this process by finishing this sentence: _____ (name) is _____ (adjective).

2. Next, place a check mark next to each adjective that applies to you as well. This is a bit more challenging because we rarely see ourselves clearly. For us to even be able to judge another, we must assume that we aren't doing that which we are judging. However, all of our judgments are about *us*, so you need to ask yourself if there is *anywhere* in your life that this (adjective) could be true of you.

Turn each of your judgments on yourself (*with kindness and grace*) and ask yourself, "If it is true that my partner is merely a reflection of me, then…:"

When am I selfish?

How am I controlling?

Where am I irresponsible?

What do I hold on to that I could share with others?

Where do I have pride?

When do I get angry?

When have I been thoughtful or kind?

Do I feel peaceful?

(or, whatever adjectives you used to describe the judgments you have about your partner)

Did you find out some things about yourself you didn't see before, My Friend? Keep in mind that this is actually a perfect setup for our healing or completeness *if* we understand the design.

I feel a strong need to emphasize a point here: Do NOT judge yourself as bad or wrong. One of the strategies of avoiding internal work or self-improvement is to place judgments on ourselves.

Example:

If I judge my partner as being selfish, i.e.: *he/she* does what *he/she* wants to do instead of what *I* want *him/her* to do (Are you smiling yet?), then I realize that I too am selfish, and my tendency will be to go even further into self-judgment, "Not only am I selfish, but I'm prideful, and judgmental, and critical, and angry, I'm a piece of sh- - t!" When we do this, we get stuck on our own judgments about how horrible we are, we take on shame, and then spiral downward into a depression because we are "bad" and we never get around to addressing our wounds.

This exercise is not intended to have you lift the judgments you hold on your partner, just to turn you around and prompt you to judge yourself! It is an exercise to raise your awareness that your partner is a *gift* who can teach you many things about yourself and facilitate your own healing. This is also an opportunity to release your judgments of your partner, and anyone else, so you can fully *Love* him/her because you discover that you and your partner are not so different after all.

I discovered that once I saw *myself* in those I judged, my judgments of them fell away and I was able to *Love* and support them in the ways I longed to be *Loved* and supported—without criticism, judgments, or the need to change them so *I* could feel better. This is what I believe the Golden Rule is all about, *"Do unto others as you would have them do unto you."* We all long to be *Loved* and accepted—warts and all! We long for others to see past our messiness and weaknesses into our beautiful *Spirit*. We need to be able to grow at our own rate, address our weaknesses at our own rate, for our own best interest as well as for others. Remember, My Friend, the best gift we can give our partner is the pursuit of our own physical, emotional, and *Spiritual* healing, health, and happiness.

Dropping our judgments is quite easy to do once you recognize that we are *all* the same; we *all* miss the mark in one way or another, we *all* need/want grace for those misses, and we *all* need to be *Loved* in spite of those misses. This is true humility: identifying with the strengths *and* weaknesses of the human race. Given the right circumstances, we are *all* capable of the most heinous crimes. We are desperate for grace, lots and lots of grace; we are *One* and the same!

If you want to be happy, stop judging *everyone, including yourself*. My point for doing this exercise is so you can see that your partner is a *gift* that *you* attracted because *you* need to be whole and *you* can't be whole without having *your* buttons pushed, without a clear reflection of yourself to observe, without changing *your* perspective, and without healing *your* wounds.

According to the teaching of *A Course In Miracles,* a miracle occurs every time we experience a shift in perspective from man's thoughts to God's thoughts. This "miracle" can also be identified as a shift from *fear to Love* because it's our fears which cause us to judge others and to try to control others. Fear is responsible for more poor choices and breakdowns in relationships than any other factor. Franklin Delano Roosevelt said in his inaugural speech, *"The only thing we have to fear is fear itself."* I wonder if he realized how far and wide that statement applied to our lives.

According to Raymond Holliwell in his book, *Working With The Law,* *"We attract that which we require."* I assert that what we require is to be healed. For some of us, that means much more suffering before we begin to investigate the actual source of our pain—which, by the way, Dear Friend, is your *story*. Oh, and, that *story* is a lie. I will expound on that principle in Section 3.

What this law of attraction means, My Friend, is that the person you call your lover is actually a wonderful *gift* or opportunity for you to address some wounds in *your* life that have been causing you a great deal of suffering, that *you* have been unaware. It's your wounds that have been limiting *your* growth and happiness, not your lover. That man or woman who is currently pushing all of your emotional "buttons," providing tons of evidence to support your *story*, making you wonder *what* you were ever attracted to in the first place, *is your gift!*

I want you to understand that all relationships last, "Until death do us part;" the "death" of the *relationship* is what causes us to leave! *Our* approach to cultivating intimate, *Loving* relationships isn't a guarantee that the relationship will last forever. For each person in a relationship plays a role in that outcome, and we have no control over what the other person chooses to do or not to do. *Our* approach does, however, greatly increase the chances of a lasting romance, especially if you are in a new relationship. *Our* approach will significantly increase *your* happiness, peacefulness, and personal power. *Our* approach is a way to receive and appropriate the beautiful gift each person is in our lives. *Our* approach is for *your* healing and growth and for those who are ready to receive from you what you have learned.

Example:

Sharon was a client of mine who was miserable and ready to walk out of her 30-year marriage. Her husband didn't participate in our coaching sessions, although my client did share what she was learning with him. Sharon assured me that her husband didn't *get* what she was sharing with him and he didn't change a thing; she did! After only a few coaching sessions with Sharon, and her working through some of these concepts, I asked her how she was doing in her marriage. She told me she was happy and could easily see herself staying in her marriage without anything more needing to change. The only thing that changed was *her* approach and *her* perspectives. Sharon now has powerful tools to remove her from her suffering mindset into a place of real peace and more freedom than she had ever known in her marriage.

I believe it is impossible to heal without these intimate relationships. I know a man who didn't want to experience the struggles of being in a close relationship again, so he eventually closed himself off to every relationship. He has not grown or healed since then. He is by far the most lonely, unhappy, and miserable man I have ever known.

Let me make this very clear: I am not suggesting that anyone stay in an abusive relationship. It is your responsibility to choose healthy people in your life. If, as you experience more and more healing, you realize you are in an unhealthy relationship, you will probably want to pause or end that relationship if they aren't willing to do their own healing work. Certainly do not place yourself in harm's way!

Here is a list of the most common *stories* we adopt from our childhood experiences which will help you answer some of the questions below:

I'm invisible

Other people are more important than me

I'm insignificant

I don't matter

I'm powerless

I have to be the responsible one

I must be in control

I'm bad

I'm a failure

I'm a mistake

Something is wrong with me

The world is unsafe

People can't be trusted

I'm not enough (probably the most common denominator of all stories)

There isn't enough (scarcity mentality; not enough money, love, food, stuff, happiness)

I'm too much (be quiet)

I'm stupid

Relationships don't last

I'm unlovable

I'm too sensitive

I'm ugly

I need a college degree to be respected or have value

I must be perfect to be accepted

I must perform so others will like me

I will never be successful

I don't deserve success

I don't deserve to be loved

I don't deserve to be happy

*SECRET INGREDIENT 2 CONCEPT: *The Partner You Have Attracted Is Your Gift*

1. We attract what we require

2. We attract our wounded equal

3. Our partner is a mirror of our strengths and weaknesses

4. Our partner is our best teacher

FAN THE FLAME

1. Which *stories* are governing your life today (see list above)? Which childhood wounds are being revealed in your current relationship?

2. What is your partner here to teach you about yourself? (Refer to the Mirror Exercise 1 - Judgments as well as your *stories*)

3. What did you learn about yourself that you didn't know before you did the Mirror Exercise?

4. In what ways do you now see that your partner is your healer?

*For additional support: If you are having difficulty identifying your childhood *stories,* your judgments, why you have attracted your partner, and/or what your partner is in your life to teach you, check out my coaching options at www.denisedarlene.com

> *Dear God of All— In All, I am grateful for the gift of healing You have brought into my life through my lover. Open my eyes to see all the ways my lover is a mirror of what I am blind to see in my own character. I promise to honor this special relationship and to allow my lover to teach me all that I can learn from him/her.*
>
> *And so it is, My Friend, and so it is!*

.

Recipe Part 2

BLEND PURPOSE WITH A NEW PERSPECTIVE

My Friend, have you ever noticed how radically different a recipe can taste with just a few changes to the ingredients? Take scrambled eggs for example. Add onion, diced peppers, chorizo, chili powder, and cheese, and you get a delicious Mexican egg scramble. Take those same scrambled eggs and add asparagus, salami, artichokes, and feta cheese for a yummy Greek scramble. Or a simple ham and cheese for a Denver scramble. Changing the lenses of our perspectives will give us an entirely different emotional experience. I absolutely love this process, and I use it whenever I want to change my perspective from fear to *Love*.

SECRET INGREDIENT 3

A NEW PERSPECTIVE ON EVENTS

"The eye is the lamp of the body; so if your eye is clear [spiritually perceptive], your whole body will be full of light [benefiting from God's precepts]. But if your eye is bad [spiritually blind], your whole body will be full of darkness [devoid of God's precepts]. So if the [very] light inside you [your inner self, your heart, your conscience] is darkness, how great and terrible is that darkness!"
Matthew 6:22-23 AMP

If it is indeed true that all *events are neutral* (and it is true), then why in the world would we interpret an *event* in such a way that we would cause ourselves and others so much suffering? For the simple reason that most of us are *unaware* of *this concept*. What we don't know *can* and does hurt us, as well as those we *Love*. Our *interpretations of events* support us being *right* about our *stories* and our judgments. It is human nature to want to be right!

When I introduced Joe to the concept of, "events are neutral," he was in total agreement. Many times since then I have observed Joe *choosing* to suffer over various events, such as his computer crashing, slow traffic, feeling disrespected, etc., I would remind him that the *event* is actually neutral and that he is responsible for his own suffering. I then would ask him if he wanted to continue to suffer or not. He would think for a moment, then very honestly say that he preferred to suffer a while longer. You gotta love an honest man!

Joe's answer raised my awareness even more to this phenomenon: The reason we continue to suffer is that there is some payoff. After observing my own *chosen* suffering many times, I now believe that payoff is a two-sided coin. On one side is our brain chemistry needing a *fix* to supply the neuron receptors the hormones they crave. The other side is a strategy to get the attention/affection we feel we need, but either don't want to ask for or don't recognize on a conscious level that we need attention.

Let's face it, a person who is visibly sad or upset gets attention. Those of us observing the person who is upset usually want to rescue them from their pain, so we ask questions, offer advice, offer a distraction, anything to stop the suffering because when a loved one suffers, we suffer too. We aren't designed to suffer; we are designed to be happy; that is our most natural, authentic self!

Whenever you notice your loved one suffering a negative emotion, it is helpful to ask them if they are aware of a fear present. If you are conscious enough to witness your own negative feelings, tell your lover which fear you are noticing. Recently, Joe helped me discover more of my *I don't matter story* buried deep within my subconscious. I'm going to share this story with you mostly because I want you to understand that the temptation to judge and control is part of our human nature, even for someone like me, who has been doing this work for many years. Doing this work requires clarity and consciousness, so practice, practice, practice, my Friend!

Example:

I was filling out a DMV registration form for Joe so he could pay our car registration online. One of the security questions was, "Which city did you meet your spouse/significant other?" Joe answered, "Irvine." Well, guess what? Joe didn't meet *me* in Irvine; that's where he met his ex-wife. I immediately felt Joe's response stomp on my *I don't matter* button, and I succumbed to the emotion of fear. While I was aware enough to understand what was happening, I wasn't conscious enough to ask Joe for his help to clarify what he meant by his response; I only wanted to bolt from my fear! I knew that *my* response wasn't about Joe. I knew Joe would never intentionally hurt my feelings or diminish *our* relationship in any way. My pain wasn't about Joe; it was about activating my *story.* What I noticed was that I immediately wanted to feel empowered, to try to control the situation—what I made up about the situation; the *situation* was neutral.

I removed myself from Joe to take myself through the four steps of *Holy Healing.* I accepted and welcomed the fear. I asked *Love* a series of questions and learned that my fear was about security and control. If you think about the reality of "security" or "control," these concepts are illusions—except in relationship to *God.* My Friend, this is where things might seem to be unclear. What I am suggesting is to get to a place where you trust in, and rest in, this "*God* of *Love*" that we can't see, touch, or hear (audibly). The ability to trust this *Source* is learned through many different experiences throughout our life, so if you are just beginning on this *Spiritual* journey, I strongly recommend you pay close attention to what it is you are hoping for, praying for, or desiring and observe the *Answer* to those requests in the many forms *They* take.

Once I recognized the source of my fear, I simply replaced the lies I was scaring myself with for the *truth.* As soon as I started writing the *truth* down in my journal, my anxiety subsided, my sadness lifted, and my peace was restored...except...I was pissed at myself for allowing myself to slide down that slippery slope of doubt, into a muddy pool of fear! I spent the next hour chastising myself for reacting to that damn button. "Oh wait! I'm doing it again!" Rather than accept my *Spiritual* growth and healing, I caused myself even more suffering by judging it. My Friend, please don't do this to yourself; it's dumb, and it doesn't serve you in any capacity!

Now, let me tell you what I wished I had done in this particular situation. I wish I would have allowed myself to be completely vulnerable with Joe and shared with him that my *story* was triggered, and I was feeling insecure; a hug from Joe would have fixed everything at that moment. I'm confident that *Love* will give me another opportunity to have those results. We get to go again, and again, until we learn the lesson and heal our *stories*. And this, My Friend, is a beautiful thing! We must all recognize by now that *Love* is far more committed to our growth than to our comfort.

Before I understood this concept, I would use suffering to get my need for attention met. I distinctly recall the day I recognized this strategy I was employing and told my then-husband, Tim, "From now on, whenever you see me upset, please ask me what I'm afraid of." That one question became a place of *grounding* for me. When Tim would ask me what I was afraid of, I was able to immediately shift to the real issue: my fear! It makes a person feel much less vulnerable to blame another or to suffer alone than to ask someone to help you calm your *fears*. Just the statement, "I'm afraid" made me feel incredibly vulnerable because I didn't want to give people an opportunity to judge me as weak. It would serve you well to pause here and watch a TED Talk by Brene Brown on "The Power of Vulnerability" at www.ted.com.

Sometimes I tell Joe when I'm feeling fearful. His response is so beautiful—and healing. He will invite me to tell him what I'm afraid of, and then listen as I go through the healing process of *Holy Healing*. He will draw me in close to his chest, wrap his arms around me, and run his fingers through my hair while he comforts me with the powerful *truth* of the present moment. That tenderness and *truth* returns me to a place of peace, and my mind is restored to sanity. Along with going through the process of healing together, Joe's tenderness is an opportunity for me to be vulnerable with him, which draws us even closer together. This close bond is very safe and liberating for me—something I had longed for all of my life.

In my relationship with Tim, I did what I see most people doing. I thought my suffering was because of someone or something outside of myself, and my reactions were the same as nearly everyone else: I blamed him/her/them/it, and I tried to get him/her/them/it to change so *I* could be happy. That's a hamster wheel, Darling; the only place it will get you is frustrated, and likely single. What I am sharing with you here works beautifully to become a truly happy, peaceful, fulfilled person.

Now that I understand that *events are neutral,* and I alone place the interpretation on every *event,* on every conversation or statement, on every other person's choices, I have the power to *choose* an interpretation that best supports my healing, happiness, *and* my relationships. Remember, My Friend, awareness illuminates choices.

*F*or now, the majority of my suffering is over because I have brought the light of *truth* to the *stories* that used to cause me to suffer so much. Now, whenever my peace or joy are disturbed, I recognize that I have automatically interpreted the *event* through a *story* to match a fear that has been present in my mind for many years.

Knowledge *applied* is power, My Friend! I want you to be powerful, so I strongly recommend you learn as much as you can about the powerhouse between your ears if you want to gain control over your life and empower your relationships. One of the best resources for you to easily understand what is going on in your brain is to watch the movie, *What The Bleep Do We Know?* You can also read up on how our brains govern much of what we automatically choose to do from the Applied Neuroscience Institute at http://www.appliedneuroscienceinstitute.com.

*SECRET INGREDIENT 3 CONCEPTS: *Events Are Neutral*

1. We automatically choose an interpretation which best support our *stories*.

2. We suffer because of our interpretations rather than because of an event.

3. We can change from suffering to joy in a moment by changing our *story*.

FAN THE FLAME

1. Reinterpret each of your childhood *stories* as you identified in SECRET INGREDIENT 2 - THE PURPOSE OF ATTRACTION

2. Choose an event (person or circumstance) you are currently suffering from and see how many different interpretations you can create for the same event. You may want to ask someone close to you to help you with this process if you get stuck. Then, choose the interpretation which empowers you and causes a shift from fear to *Love*, from despair to hope, from pain to peace.

3. If you are suffering as a result of someone else's choices, tell the story from their perspective in the first person (as if you were them).

Dear God of All— In All, I have some childhood wounds that have been clouding my perspective and limiting my joy. Please reveal to me all of those stories that have been hindering my capacity to Love myself and others as You Love us. Lastly, give me eyes to see and ears to hear everything and everyone as You do. Help me discover the perspective of Love in all things.

And so it is, My Friend, and so it is!

SECRET INGREDIENT 4

A NEW PERSPECTIVE ON EMOTIONAL BUTTONS

The Spirit of God, the Master, is upon me, because God anointed me. He sent me to preach good news to the poor. To heal the heartbroken, announce freedom to all captives, pardon all prisoners. God sent me to announce the year of his grace—a celebration of God's destruction of our enemies— and to comfort all who mourn. To care for the needs of all who mourn in Zion, give them bouquets of roses instead of ashes, Messages of joy instead of news of doom, a praising heart instead of a languid spirit.
Isaiah 61:1-7 MSG

When baking a cake or making a sauce, it is critical that all of the lumps in the batter or roux are smoothed out for a delicious recipe. No one wants to bite into a clump of flour! Every cook knows that all of the dry ingredients must be thoroughly mixed into the recipe, or it simply won't turn out well. The same is true for these relationship "ingredients." All of them are significant in their own right, but blended together they make a magnificent relationship recipe!

Our emotions are a brilliant, useful resource if we understand their designs and functions. Our emotions let us know if we are having fearful thoughts or *Loving* thoughts. In the same way that physical pain lets us know that something is wrong with our body that requires our attention, emotional pain lets us know there is something wrong in our thinking/believing that also requires our attention.

Dear Friend, imagine with me for a moment what life would be like without any *emotional buttons* or negative *stories* to confirm or react to. What would life be like for you if you were never offended? If you didn't take anything personally and just let the irregular behavior of other people roll right on by you without a twinge of irritation? How happy would you feel? How free would you feel? Do you think that is even possible, My Friend?

I'm here to tell you that it IS possible, My Friend. I am now aware of all of the *buttons* that I used to unconsciously react to. Those *buttons* no longer have power in my life; I do! I realize that I have a *choice* about what I think and feel. I am able to dismiss fear quickly each time it comes up as I take the experience through the healing process of *Holy Healing*. This doesn't mean that I don't have any buttons or that I never experience negative emotions; I do! But they are few, brief, and far between. Now, whenever a button is pushed, it only takes a few moments to shift from fear to *Love,* and to restore internal peace.

My Friend, our preconceived perceptions, based on our personal life experiences, are the lenses through which we view life. *Our* lenses [perspectives] are not the *whole truth*, the *only truth*, and *nothing but the truth*; they are simply *our truth*, which many times couldn't be further from *the truth*! I assert that those thoughts which we hold as *truth,* which cause us so much suffering, are, in reality, lies. These lies need to be brought into the light of our awareness, examined, identified as lies, and replaced with the *truth* of *Love*.

Whenever you have a negative emotion (have your *button* pushed through either something someone said or did, or a particular situation), it's important **not** to dismiss that feeling or pretend it doesn't matter; **it does matter** because it's letting you know that something is amiss within. It is actually pointing at your *story,* which happens to be a *lie* you hold as *the* truth (refer to the list of *stories* in the previous chapter). Therefore, first, simply notice and identify the emotion. It's kind of like getting a knock on the door and opening it to identify who's there. It may be anger, or anxiety, or sadness, or hopelessness, or powerlessness. Whatever the negative feeling is, I assert it has the same source—FEAR! Fear is the result of believing or entertaining a *lie* as though it were the truth.

How do I know that what you *believe,* which causing you so much suffering, really *is* a lie? Because Dear One, those *stories* we hold to be the truth with a capital "T" were *events* which took place when we were children, and as *children,* we decided what those *events* meant. Or the event is being processed with limited information or insight leading to a faulty interpretation. However, as I taught you in the previous chapter, *events are actually neutral;* the interpretation is a personal perspective—in this case, the perspective of a child or the result of partial information.

Now I ask you, My Friend, what does a child know about life or people that they can accurately interpret what happens to them as children?

Example:

Let's go back to my *stories* of "I don't matter" and, "Everybody leaves me." As a 6-year-old child, I decided that the *events* of my father leaving, my brother being put into foster care, and my mother sending us to live across the country were facts about the way the world *is.* I made my father's choice to abandon his children about me. It never occurred to me, at the age of six, that my father's choices were about *him*. Now, I know differently! Now, I know the truth! Of course, his choice to leave his children was about *him* for whatever wounds he carried from his past; he wasn't raised right either! However, merely *knowing* the truth about my father wasn't enough to break free from a lifetime of not only believing that *I didn't matter* but a lifetime of gathering evidence (my interpretations) from *event* after *event* that *I don't matter*. This process of healing takes time, My Friend; heck, it takes time just to realize we are reacting to our *story* every time a *button* gets pushed. So, be very patient.

Science, yes, *science*, has confirmed that our brains are in a constant search for being happy, but our *stories* from our childhood perspective cause us to be unhappy. The obvious *work* then is to interrupt the *lie* that is causing us to suffer and replace it with the *Truth*. Does that make sense, My Friend?

Tony Robbins says, "We can have our *story*, or our *story* can have us." When we react to various triggers, that is our *story* having us. When we go through the process of *Holy Healing*, we remove those triggers so that our old *stories* no longer have any power in our lives. With *Holy Healing*, we are actually creating a new *story*, a new belief to filter our experiences through and govern our choices by. It's not enough to drop the old *stories*, we must replace them entirely.

Unfortunately, what most people do is try to *control* the unwanted behavior in their partner so *they* can feel better. Controlling others is the way we tear down our relationships; it doesn't work and never has! And yet, we do it over and over again, generation after generation— totally missing what has been destroying the passion, *Love*, fun, and security of our most intimate relationships.

Example:

Linda was asking advice about her husband Bill's "improper behavior" in public; apparently, he would burp during a meal. Linda wanted to know how she could get Bill to *behave* in public.

The *problem* according to Linda is her husband's inappropriate and rude behavior in public. Keep in mind this *event is neutral;* Linda *decided* what it meant. In some cultures, burping after a meal is a sign of respect and a compliment to the cook. Linda's *interpretation* was causing her, and Bill, a great deal of suffering.

I wonder if *you* can hear the problem in Linda's *story*, or Linda's *story* in this problem. If you struggle with the same *story*, then you probably *agree* with Linda and can't imagine why I'm saying that Linda's approach is even an issue. After all, this husband is misbehaving and embarrassing the hell out of poor Linda!

Let's unpack this situation. First, it is inappropriate to correct another adult, PERIOD! Correcting, complaining, nagging, or punishing is an attempt to control others. Dr. William Glasser calls these behaviors, "external control" and says that 99.99% of the population uses this approach in an effort to be happy. Trust me, My Friend, when I tell you it is a death sentence to any relationship if you use any kind of control behaviors. The very need to control situations or people is a response to fear. Fear is destructive to you and to those you are in a relationship with. I will expand this concept from Dr. Glasser's book *Choice Theory* in Secret Ingredient 7.

Second, it is emasculating to correct any man, especially in public! The fastest way to a failed relationship is to emasculate a man. Don't do it! If your partner is a man, you must remember that he is NOT your child, even if he behaves like one. No one wants to sleep with their mother; it's gross. Who we want to sleep with is our partner, our companion, our best friend, our lover. I will talk more about what men and women need most in relationships in Section 5.

Back to Linda: The questions I explored with Linda are: "Why is Bill's behavior a problem for *you?*" "Which *button* is being pushed in *you?*" Ultimately, "What are *you* afraid of?." Turns out, it was a *story* about being judged for not being perfect, performing, giving the illusion that her family has it all together, that her husband was raised right, and making sure *they* look good to avoid being judged. Avoiding being judged is a survival strategy for Linda. She believes that she isn't enough if she isn't perfect; her underlying *story* is, "I'm not enough" or, "If I'm not perfect, then I will be judged and rejected." Can you see how exhausting it would be for Linda to try to micromanage everyone close to her so *she* isn't judged as "not enough" or run the risk of being rejected?

The *healing* work for Linda is to discover what her real fears are, interrupt the *story,* and reinterpret it, NOT to correct her husband! Trust me, someone else will bring, or already has brought, this to Bill's attention. *He* will change when the behavior becomes a problem for *him*—and that, like it or not, is Bill's business, not Linda's! Bill, unbeknownst to Linda, is a *gift* for her, not a problem. Bill's behavior launches an attack on Linda's fears, drawing the *lies* of her *story* up to the surface where *she* can investigate *her* judgments and fears. If Linda took her judgments of her husband through the Mirror Exercise, she might have judged Bill as being rude and disrespectful. But wasn't Linda being rude and disrespectful by correcting her husband in public? And wasn't Linda being judgmental, as she feared she would be judged? "Yes" is the answer to those questions! This is a perfect *event* which can result in *healing,* freedom, and more *Love* for Linda and for her husband given this awareness and these tools.

Please keep in mind Dear One, this special most intimate relationship must be the one place in the world where your partner feels safe and is able to work out his/her misses in life without criticism, complaining, or feeling like he/she isn't enough. *This* is the relationship where our *Spirits* are celebrated and our egos are ignored, where our strengths are encouraged, where we *model* for each other what works, where we observe without criticism what doesn't work, and where we heal *our* own emotional buttons.

Whenever my clients tell me their partners keep pushing their *buttons*, I just smile and say, "Well then, let's get rid of those *buttons,* shall we, Dear?" I always begin with the Mirror Exercise to get them out of their partner's business and onto their own issues. The look on their faces is priceless, as they were expecting me to side with them and tell them how right they are and how their partners needs to change. Nope! Our partners don't need to change a thing; but, if *we* want to be happy, we can take that painful opportunity, look deep inside to see what just got touched by our partner's behavior, and take *that* to *Spirit* within for some *Truth* so we can be set free and healed.

My Friend, other people are not responsible for our happiness any more than we are responsible for the happiness of others; we are each responsible for our own happiness! We are happy or not because we have *decided* to be happy, or not, AND we have done the work of *healing,* or not!

Keep in mind, Dear One, that just because you understand, and may even agree with these concepts, changing life-long beliefs and behaviors does not come easily or without resistance. As I already said, our brains are addicted to repetitive, dominant emotions. You will literally be *forcing* your brain to think different thoughts until those new, healthy thoughts and brain hormones become a natural condition through healthy, loving, repetitious thought patterns. This is the same process of repetitive thoughts that got you to where you are now. You are literally going to wash your brain of those nasty viruses that have been clogging up your thinking, emotions, and behaviors.

Sacred writings teach that we are so busy pointing out what's wrong with others we have not managed our own affairs. The *truth* is, we have so much personal work to do on our own character and *emotional buttons*. If we were to mind our own business, we would hardly even notice when others are messing up. I'm pretty sure the main reason we butt our noses into other people's business is that it's a great distraction from our own issues. It's much easier to point out what isn't working for other people than to figure out how to heal ourselves; it's also far less painful to be in someone else's mess than to look closely at our own.

Whenever I notice something is out of order in Joe's life, I immediately ask myself, "Who's business is this: mine, his, or *God's?*" Guess whose business it never is? Yup, mine! My next question is, "Where do I see this behavior in my life?" 100 percent of the time I am able to find that behavior in my own life; Joe becomes the *gift* in that moment rather than the problem. I don't need to correct *him* to be happy, I need to correct *me*! Immediately, I am able to have grace for his behavior because I GET IT! I GET IT because I'VE GOT IT! I receive the *gift* of reflection (Mirror Exercise) and get to work on my issue. When Joe is ready, he can work on his own issue. Until then, I get to share with him what I have discovered about *myself,* and I get to be a light for him as he watches me heal, grow, and become empowered. Can you see how beautiful this relationship can be? How non-threatening? How empowering? How healing?

Example:

Recently, Joe was helping me process through my ongoing resistance to exercising. He was trying to get at the core of my resistance. I shared with him that it isn't the discomfort. I actually feel better when I exercise. It's the time it takes to see results relative to the time I have to invest. He wasn't connecting to my reasoning, so I said, "It's kind of like the resistance you have to writing the book you've been talking about since I met you. It's going to take a while to write that book, but the results of writing and speaking are exactly what you say you deeply desire." When I drew the parallel between my resistance and his, he got it! AND I got it! Joe has been working on his book since that conversation.

Please keep in mind, My Friend your partner, may or may not join you on this healing journey. He/she may or may not care, or pay any attention to, the transformation taking place in you; that is not your business either! However, the results will be that *you* are elevating, becoming whole, experiencing more happiness, enjoying more peace, enabling yourself to *Love* better, and developing more grace for others and for yourself. It's a wonderful way to live your life! I promise!

FAN THE FLAME

MIRROR EXERCISE 2 - "SHOULD'S"

1. What do you see in your partner that he/she *should* be doing or not doing? What do you nag or complain about? What do you blame him/her for?

2. What do you see clearly that your partner doesn't seem to be aware of?

3. What is it that you *should* be doing or not doing?

4. What has now opened up for you? What are you now aware of?

Emotional buttons are evidence that our *story* has been triggered. These *buttons* are like shells or pits which must be removed (healed) for us to be able to experience the degree of happiness, peace, and *Love* we all long for. I learned a powerful healing technique from Father Thomas Keating through Contemplative Outreach, which he calls, "Welcoming Prayer." I took Fr. Keating's approach to *Spiritual* healing and combined it with several other concepts to provide a system of healing and empowerment that I refer to as *Holy Healing*. I encourage you to check out Fr. Keating's material at http://www.contemplativeoutreach.org.

The word *Holy* as I am using it here refers to being *Spiritually* whole, complete, lacking nothing, and aligned with *truth* (right thinking). *Holy Healing* takes place as a result of consulting with, and responding to, our *Inner Guide*. Some people call this *Inner Guide God, Holy Spirit, Divine Presence, Universal Energy*, etc. Some people don't believe in a higher *Intelligence* at all, much less that "He" lives in individuals or speaks to people; they refer to this *Inner Guide* as their *Intuition*. It really doesn't matter what your beliefs are, or which terminology you prefer; as long as you do the work, you will find healing taking place in your inner life. Your increasing sense of happiness and peace are the *fruit* of your *Spiritual* healing.

Whenever my peace is disturbed, I take myself through this process of healing that I am sharing with you here. Once I have turned my perspective from fearful thoughts, which are causing me to suffer, into *Loving* thoughts, my peace is restored.

HOLY HEALING

Awareness, Acceptance, Application, and Alchemy.

Below, I will explain each step and give examples, then I will take you through an example of how all the steps work together as I process my own buttons.

HEALING STEP 1: AWARENESS

We cannot change what we are unaware of. I assert that all of our problems come from this foundation of blindness or being totally unaware of ourselves at a deep emotional, physical, and *Spiritual* level. We are trained in Western society to silence symptoms. The Western approach to medicine is a perfect example of attacking *symptoms* rather than healing the underlying cause of dis-ease. America is a drug-focused country rather than a wellness-focused country; "Make me *feel* well rather than *be* well. Relieve my pain, rather than restore my health."

Through this material, I am raising your awareness to your deepest emotional dis-ease, those negative emotions that get triggered by an event, a comment, or behavior so that you can begin to address the real hindrance to your happiness. We don't need new people or circumstances to be happy any more than we need new medicine to be healthy. As a matter of fact, you will find yourself in the exact same condition of illness and unhappiness regardless of the pills you take or the people you are with because you aren't addressing the real problem.

Can you see why our emotions are such a beautiful design? Getting our buttons triggered is the *only* way out of suffering and into happiness. This is so contrary to what we have been taught!

This process of healing *through* awareness could also be accurately called, *Emotional Intervention* because we are quite addicted to not only our *stories* but also to the hormones released by the automatic reaction those *stories* produce in our brains. Our brains actually *need* a fix of the hormones produced by our emotions. Eckhart Tolle teaches that we all have a "pain body ego" which requires suffering to survive so it continually seeks adversity. I strongly recommend reading *A New Earth* to become aware of this part of our human experience.

Breaking away from the pattern of self-suffering can be as challenging as breaking away from any other substance abuse. That may sound absurd to you right now, but just wait until you start putting this process into practice.

Awareness brings power and choice like nothing else in our lives!

HEALING STEP 2: ACCEPTANCE

Let's go deeper into the *healing* practice, shall we, My Friend? So far I have taught you to recognize any negative feelings triggered by an event: a comment, behavior, or a circumstance you *perceive* as a problem. Next, as soon as you tune into your feelings, identify which feeling is haunting you and find where it is in your body. Put your hand on that part of your body as if you are holding the pain and feel it as deeply as possible saying, "Oh _____ (fear, anxiety, despair, anger, etc.), it's you. Let's see what you are here to teach me." What we resist persists; so, if you are going to experience healing, you must acknowledge and welcome both the experience *and* the emotions. What's different about this healing practice than, say, traditional psychology, is that you aren't just going to accept the negative emotion and allow yourself to *feel* those feelings, and you aren't going to look for, or blame, anyone in your past for *causing* those negative feelings. You *are* going to go deeper and investigate which *thoughts* or *stories* are triggering those negative feelings.

HEALING STEP 3: APPLICATION

We do not suffer because of anything outside of us; we suffer because of our *thoughts* or *our interpretation* of what happens outside of us. Those *thoughts* are fear-based lies, and that is what is causing us to suffer, My Friend.

Negative feelings are actually perceived *fears* we have about our security, belonging (approval & acceptance), control, freedom, or value. We suffer because at some level we believe a *lie* about those basic needs being met, currently or in the future.

According to Dr. Glasser, when our basic human needs are met to the degree we require them, we call this state of being "Happy." Dr. Glasser identifies those needs as (1) *Love and Belonging (2) Security (3) Control (4) Freedom (5) Fun.* If we perceive that one or more of these needs are not being met to the degree that we believe we need them to be met, we call this state, "Suffering." Is it true that those needs are not being met? Who said our needs aren't being met? We did! What if that's not true? What if all of our needs are always fulfilled to some degree, and we are merely projecting lack into the future? Here we can look closely at the *fear* or the *lie* that is driving our emotional state and ask ourselves, "Is it true?" or "Is there more I'm not seeing?"

Example:

I recently experienced the gift of being able to reframe a challenging situation from a limited perspective to a much bigger picture that has completely transformed my emotions, energy, and joy regarding this particular need being met; the need is *belonging*. When I was growing up, my "family" consisted of my mother and older brother much of the time. We moved away from the rest of our family when I was a baby. I had no grandparents, aunts, uncles, or cousins around. As I dreamed of creating my own family someday, I knew I wanted a close extended family. Tim and I had three sons, we lived close to my brother and his three daughters, Tim's sister and her three children lived 4 miles away, and his parents were 15 minutes away. We were together a lot, and I loved the sense of *belonging* that I experienced during those precious years.

After my divorce in 2013, many of those relationships ended. I have suffered a lot of sadness over the loss of *belonging* to a family the past three years. One day I was processing with Joe a disappointment about my boys canceling a barbecue that I had been looking forward to (by now you must know which *story* that event triggered). I felt *Spirit* invite me to expand my perspective of "family." Rather than believing that *my family* was limited to my relatives, I awakened to the fact that *my family* is extended to the entire human race. The reality is, I have many young people who call me "Momma D" whom I *Love* and enjoy as much as the children I gave birth to. I have many friends I call brothers and sisters that I *Love* as deeply as I do my dear sweet older brother. And there are a few older people who have been like a mother and father in my life. *My family* is huge! They are everywhere I go. I literally *belong* to everyone! I'm never without family around me, and this perspective deeply satisfies my need for *belonging!* As my week unfolded I had several opportunities to have conversations with *my family.* With each call, I felt more and more *Love* and gratitude for this beautiful family that I *belong* to. The only thing that changed to bring me from a place of sadness to joy and fulfillment was *my* perspective. What if all of our needs are already and always met, and all we need to do is make a slight adjustment to our perspective to be more fulfilled and joyful?

Once you have become aware of your negative emotion, named it, and welcomed it, you then find in your body where you are feeling that emotion and put your hand on it. You then find which basic human need is being threatened by asking yourself (or *Spirit*), "Is this about my security, belonging, control, freedom, or my value?" You will know which need is being threatened immediately as soon as you say it out loud. Whenever I do this exercise, my negative emotion intensifies when I say the need (like, belonging) that is being threatened.

HEALING STEP 4: ALCHEMY

After you have accepted the fear-based emotion, located the feeling in your body, and identified which basic human need feels threatened, you are going to take *your interpretation* of the event for some *Holy Healing*. You are going to first identify the fear-thought driving the emotion and call it what it is—a *lie*! It's not important that you believe it's a lie right now, just agree with me that it is a *lie* and move on to the next step.

Next, replace that *lie* with the *truth*, which will be the exact opposite of what you are currently believing. In my case, whenever I believe the *lie* that *I don't matter,* I merely tell myself that I *do* matter and I will recount as many people as possible to whom I matter, including myself and God.

Once you have interrupted the *fear/lie* and replaced it with the *truth*, you will be set free from the emotions torturing your mind and your body, leaving you in a state of peace. You may need to talk yourself through this new interpretation a few times before the emotions shift. There were times when I had to tell myself over and over the many ways I matter, to whom, and why. One thing I've noticed gets me to a state of peace more quickly is to invite Joe into my process. Since I'm not blaming him in any way or trying to change anything about him, he feels safe to support me and affirm me in ways that make the biggest impact.

Do not concern yourself with immediately believing this new *truth*; you have believed a *lie* a very long time, so be patient as you turn your beliefs around. This process is more like turning the Titanic around than a row boat. You may need to repeat out loud, or write down, as many *truths* as you can think of several times to get it to stick. You can expect to do this process repeatedly before you notice that you are beginning to believe the opposite of your *story*. You will find that each time your button gets pushed it will be less intense and will take less and less time to shift your emotions from *fear to Love.*

Isn't that powerful, My Friend? Nothing and no one else needs to change for you to be happy and experience a peaceful emotional state. *You* alone possess the choice to be happy and the choice to suffer.

Example:

I used to believe that if I wasn't someone's wife, that I didn't *belong*. That belief caused me a lot of suffering at the beginning of my relationship with Joe. Since Joe didn't want to be married again, and I didn't want to continue to suffer, I decided to investigate my belief about *belonging*.

Here is the process I moved through to go from a state of *fear to Love*:

AWARENESS

I found a quiet space to still my body and my mind.

I identified the emotion I was experiencing: anxiety.

ACCEPTANCE

I found the anxiety in my body (most often anxiety is in my heart). I put my hand on my heart, took a deep breath, and said, "Oh, anxiety, it's you. Let's see what you are here to teach me."

APPLICATION

Next, I asked *Spirit within*, "What am I afraid of? Is this about my security? Is it about feeling *valuable*? Is it about *control*? Is it about my *freedom*? Is it about *belonging*?" When I asked *Spirit* if it was about *belonging*, my heart rate increased as my fear was triggered—perfect! I landed on the real issue.

ALCHEMY

Next, I asked *Spirit*, "Is it true that if I'm not married to someone that I don't *belong* to anyone?" Of course not! What is my interpretation of *belonging* anyway? I will always *belong* to God. Then, what is my deeper fear? Isn't my deep *fear* that I will be alone with no one to *Love* or be *Loved* by? Is that true? Well, only if I choose to live on an island and isolate myself from the rest of the world could that be true. As soon as I discovered what my *deepest* fear was, I was able to interrupt that *lie* and replace it with the *truth*, causing an emotional shift from *fear to Love*, from pain to peace.

In the above example of reminding myself of the *truth*, I recited as many people as I could recall who *Love* me, accept me, and with whom I matter. I was able to find that there are many relationships where I feel a deep sense of *belonging* including my relationship with Joe. My conclusion then was, "I have many *Loving* relationships, and I do *belong*; marriage has nothing to do with *belonging*."

Example:

When I was married to Tim, I felt trapped and paralyzed with fear of leaving an unhealthy relationship for several *reasons* (aka lies). Because of my need for *belonging*, I was afraid that if I left Tim, I would be judged and abandoned by family and friends—*leaving me alone*. Because of my age (53 at the time), I believed that men would always choose younger more beautiful women over me—leaving me without someone to *Love* or to *Love* me. Because of Tim's choice to abuse alcohol, I felt like my world was out of *control*. I felt like I didn't have the *freedom* to choose and *control* my own life. Was any of that true? Was I suffering because of Tim's choices or because of *mine*?

What I learned was that I had all the *freedom* and *control* I wanted and needed to make *myself* happy. My worst fears were confronted when I left Tim, in that I did experience judgments and rejection from some family and friends, but guess what? I did the work of interrupting the *lie* that I would be alone and that *I didn't matter*. I chose to have grace for the people in my life who didn't understand my choices. As a result, the most important relationships in my life have been restored, and I have met some of the loveliest people who I consider to be my family in this new chapter of my life. Also, not only did I attract an amazing man, he is beautiful, and eight years younger than me… Bonus!

My interpretation of *belonging* has changed and expanded to a belief that has given me a deeper sense of *belonging* now than I have ever had. My mind and emotions are *healed,* healthy, and happy regarding this *story.*

This is the process I take every negative emotion through to discover which fear-based lie I believe. Inviting *Spirit* to show me the *truth*, I am able to replace the *lie* with a thought which supports peace and joy in my life.

Example:

Joe is a brilliant and exceptional photographer. On one level he is able to recognize his talent, but when it comes to publishing his work, he feels quite average. Joe spends time looking at *other* photographers' work, expounding on how amazing the images are without an inkling his work is as good as, if not better than, theirs—but I see it! I have encouraged him many times to publish his work, but he continues to resist. At the writing of this book, we have minimal (albeit enough) financial resources. Joe publishing his work could really help us.

Which *button* do you think is pushed in me by Joe not working on his project? It's a security *button*: "We won't have enough money." If I didn't know better, I would nag him and complain about him not getting his work "out there." Ultimately, I would try to put *my* fear on him so *he* would be afraid too. My strategy would be to motivate him to create a way for more income so *I* could feel less fear. But I know better. That common but destructive strategy would only injure our relationship, and it wouldn't work!

What is *my* fear about anyway? The only way to discover the answer to that question would be to take it through the Holy Healing process to shed some light on it and bring some *truth* to the lie that I am somehow unsafe. I have never gone without all of my basic needs being met my entire life. I have always had a home to live in, people who *Love* me, enough fun, freedom, and control over my life. I have never even been hungry a day in my life due to finances. If my fears are security based, then what is *security* anyway? Who is responsible for *my* financial security? Just like my interpretation of *belonging* needed to be reinterpreted and expanded, so did my interpretation of *security* need to be revised.

As I probed into this fear, I discovered that my real fear was about being powerless. My deepest belief was that *I* was powerless to provide a good income for us to have the life we both enjoy. In reality, I was giving my power away to someone (anyone, everyone) I thought was more talented and had better resources to make money. Now, isn't that a big, fat lie? Of course, it is! I am equally as gifted at my craft as Joe is at his, as my ex-husband was at his, as every other successful person is at theirs. As soon as I got my mind straight and aligned with *truth,* my peace was restored.

Now, whenever I notice Joe minimizing his talents or resisting working on his own projects, that is my perfect opportunity to address *me* minimizing *my* talents and resisting working on *my* projects. I see *myself* in Joe! I see *my* fear, the lies I tell *myself, my* resistance, and *I* am motivated as a result. If I am nearly the writer/teacher that Joe is a writer/photographer, this book will be a bestseller! If Joe is a true reflection of *me* and of *my* potential, then I'm more than good enough. *I* can have an enormous financial impact for us, and *I* can have the impact on relationships that *I* long to see. I *will* create a *Real Passion Revolution*! Joe's behaviors, which triggered my *emotional button,* have now become my *gift* of *healing* and inspiration. Does that make sense, My Friend? Refer back to the Mirror Exercises to process the gift your lover is for you whenever you get stuck. If you do so, you will find the most important work that needs *your* attention—*your* fears.

I feel it necessary to interject this exception here: This healing process can be successful for every kind of suffering except for grief/ loss. While we can sometimes lessen our suffering from the loss of a person or pet by Holy Healing, I do believe that allowing ourselves to mourn the loss of Love is necessary for our healing. Just be sure you aren't adding to your suffering by a faulty belief (like, "I'll never find another soulmate/Love again"). Take your grief through the above healing process to be sure you are only grieving the loss of the person/pet no longer around to share your life with. Leave plenty of space for that sorrow whenever it shows up without any judgments that it should be different. Your suffering will lessen in time, but it shouldn't be rushed as if it's a problem.

I hope I have made this *Holy Healing* process clear for you, Dear One. I'm excited for you to gain momentum in this practice as you find yourself experiencing deeper levels of happiness, contentment, gratitude, and especially *Love.*

Remember, My Friend, you must practice these steps over and over, every time your peace or happiness is disturbed to develop the necessary brain-muscles and brain chemistry to make this process more and more your "mental-default" to facilitate your personal *healing* and happiness.

*SECRET INGREDIENT 4 CONCEPTS: *Emotional Buttons Reveal Our Wounds. Transforming Our Stories with The Holy Healing Process*

1. Heal a childhood story

2. Mirror Exercise 2 – "Should's"

3. Holy Healing Process

FAN THE FLAME

1. Consider your most recent negative emotional episode (perhaps you're experiencing one now). Take your event through the steps below and write down what you discover as you go through the *Holy Healing* process.

2. Which emotion is being triggered? Where in your body are you feeling that emotion? Welcome that feeling as you would a friend; it is here to support your healing and happiness.

3. What is the lie you have been believing that is disturbing your peace and joy? Ex.: I'm not enough. I don't matter. I'm stupid. (This is your childhood *story* being triggered. Refer to the most common childhood stories in Secret Ingredient 2 for a list if you are having difficulty defining your *story*.)

4. Which basic human need is feeling threatened by believing that lie? (security, belonging, fun, freedom, personal power/ control, or value)

5. Turn this "lie" around. What is the truth about this *story?* (Recite as many opposites of the lie you have been believing as possible)

6. How do you feel after doing this healing process?

Dear God of All— In ALL, You know, and I know that I am in need of healing. Open my eyes to discover the source of my fears and replace them with Your truth. Remind me that I am never alone, I am deeply loved, and I am secure in my world.

And so it is, My Friend, and so it is!

SECRET INGREDIENT 5

A NEW PERSPECTIVE ON FORGIVENESS

"Forgiveness is the key to happiness. Here is the answer to your search for peace"
- A Course In Miracles

My Friend, the practice of forgiveness is such a critical step in our healing, happiness, and freedom, but for some it is nearly impossible! It seems we are programmed for a form of justice that isn't true. If someone offends us we want "justice." We want "An eye for an eye, and a tooth for a tooth...," until, of course, it comes to our infractions; then we want grace, understanding, compassion, and forgiveness.

And yet, *forgiveness,* not justice, is the key to our healing and happiness. It is the answer to our search for peace. A resentful, bitter mind is full of fear, and there is no room in it for *Love* to grow. Just as light and darkness cannot coexist, neither can fear and *Love,* anger and gratitude, resistance and contentment, resentment and peace. Bitterness, anger, resistance, anxiety, hopelessness, depression, and frustration are all the fruits of a fearful mind. These negative emotions are the evidence in our lives that we lack the understanding that would cause *Love* to abound. Scripture teaches us that, "Perfect [complete] *Love* casts out all fear." Therefore, if we suffer from negative emotions our *Love* is incomplete; it is lacking. *We* misunderstand what *Love* truly is. *Love,* true *Love,* is a fountain of *Living Water;* it supports life! *Love* is always full and complete. *Love* lacks nothing. *Love* gives without loss. *Love* is an eternal supply and an abundant resource. When true *Love* is present, there is nothing to fear.

THE FOUR STAGES OF FORGIVENESS:

I assert that our degree of *awareness* (consciousness) directly correlates to these stages of forgiveness.

1. "I have to *forgive*": This perspective may come from religious beliefs that I am *commanded* to forgive someone of an offense because *God* has *forgiven* me of all of my mistakes. But this mindset is an obligation and comes from a place of obedience and self-interest (to avoid *God's* wrath), rather than from a place of understanding and grace. This type of *forgiveness* isn't *forgiveness* at all; it's more of a denial and avoidance. "If I don't think about what this person did to me then I've *forgiven* them." Nope, you haven't! Trying to forget what someone did or the pain you suffered because of someone else is not *forgiveness*; it's denial!

2. "I need to *forgive*": This belief may come from the awareness of the physical impact that bitterness has on us. I've heard it said that refusing to *forgive* someone is like drinking poison and expecting the other person to die. We may come to the awareness that as long as I continue to hold onto an offense, I am tied to that individual. While this is a letting go in one sense, it is still an obligation—strictly from a place of self-interest again.

3. "I want to *forgive*": Now we are getting somewhere! This is an expression from the heart of a person who does want to let go of an offense and perhaps has even "tried" but just can't seem to get past the pain or the perceived offense. This is the first step toward truly *forgiving* someone. This is a very honest place to be: a desire to *forgive*, without the necessary understanding to get all the way to true *forgiveness* and freedom.

4. "There is nothing to *forgive*": This is the highest level of awareness/consciousness. True *forgiveness* is treating another as if they had never betrayed you. It is the perspective of *Grace*. It is recognizing we are all in the process of *Spiritual* development where some *wounds* are more expressive than others. It is the deepest understanding of human behavior. It is the fruit of seeking *Love's* perspective of a person and their choices. It is recognizing that we are all doing our best at any given time as we react to life with all of its challenges as well as our level of awareness/growth/emotional and spiritual wellness. True *forgiveness* is natural and effortless because the choices of another are never taken personally. There is never an offense perceived, therefore, nothing to *forgive*. This was the truth spoken from the cross when Jesus said, "Father *forgive* them for they know not what they do." We can, with awareness, all experience the same perspective Jesus had and offer the same prayer for our brethren. This is *Love*, and *Love* is all that matters. *Love* is the answer to all of our suffering. *Love* wins!

My Friend, have you ever had an experience where a friend or your lover came to you and asked for *forgiveness*, but there was nothing to *forgive* from your experience? This happens to me all the time. I'm often at a loss for a response because I wasn't offended by whatever was said or done. It is my friend/partner who assumes I was hurt, likely because whatever they did or said would have offended *them*. Remember, Sweetheart, "We do not see the world as it is. We see the world as we are." What I make up is that my friend/partner needs to *forgive* themselves for their behavior. I tell them that I appreciate their request, and I affirm their courage and commitment to our relationship. But, I also assure them that I was never offended by their behavior. I want my lover and my friends to understand that there is plenty of room in our relationship for mistakes. There is plenty of grace in the bank to cover any misses with me. I have been given so much *Grace* from *Love* that I feel like no one can be as messy as I am. Therefore, everyone is covered by *Grace* in my world.

Here is the problem as I see it, My Friend: We are mostly *unaware* of our own misses, issues, and hurtful choices, similar to the way we miss that our partners are our mirror. We are so focused on how others are doing *it* wrong that we are blind to the plethora of ways in which *we* do *it* wrong. We are in the habit of minimizing, or completely dismissing, our own hurtful choices and maximizing the poor choices of others. The scales of justice are NOT equal, which is why we can hold onto an offense with so much self-righteousness. Not only do we believe someone intentionally hurt us, to support our pain and our judgments of them, but we also think they should be punished for those hurtful choices, until we see that they have suffered as much as we have; hurt people hurt people…all day long!

However, our satisfaction, happiness, and freedom are not in this kind of human standard of justice. Just ask a parent of a child that was murdered if the incarceration or death of the murderer relieved their suffering at all; it doesn't. Their child is still dead, and that loss is the pain they must suffer the remainder of their life. It is unnecessary *additional* suffering to add non-forgiveness to the pain of loss to one's life as well.

So how do we navigate through the pain and disappointments caused by others without demanding justice? How can we release, actually release, a perceived offense?

I have learned a few key perspectives which have been incredibly powerful to set me free from judging anyone. <u>If there are no judgments, there can be no offenses.</u> Therefore, no one to *forgive*.

1. Judge Not: "Father *forgive* them for they know not what they do" Luke 23:34

Let's not forget that events are neutral; be sure to examine the many possible interpretations of the event, the perceived offense, as well as the person you are judging.

Example:

After I had left my ex-husband, Tim, I encountered the judgments of several significant people in my life, including most of my family and one of my closest friends. These kind and *Loving* people made their judgments of me based on partial information. I made a choice they didn't understand, nor condone, nor want to support, based on their limited information. Rather than ask me questions, they made assumptions; so, they "sided" with Tim and distanced themselves from me. How do I know their judgments were based on limited information? Because no one asked me any questions at the time, and it would have been impossible for anyone to know many of the key components to my decision process unless they asked *me*.

Nearly a year after I left Tim, my mother asked me a few questions about my experience and the process by which I made my choice to leave Tim. Immediately after I shared *my story* she said, "Honey, I had no idea that's what was going on in your life!" To which I responded, "I know, Mom." That is why I wasn't angry with her for *her* choices. However, I was hurt, which was an opportunity for me to address my "Everybody leaves me," and "I don't matter" *stories*. I was able to stay

Loving toward mother, and my friend, because I recognized that they did not fully know what they were doing. One of the beautiful gifts of being judged by others is that it has reinforced that I never want to hurt someone by assuming I know enough to stand as their judge.

I have learned that every situation has several perspectives. There is my perspective, your perspective, and *Love's* perspective. So, it is entirely impossible for us to make a proper judgment without gathering *all* the evidence; even then, we will never really know enough to stand as another's judge. I believe this is why the scriptures admonish us to "Judge not." *God* and *God* alone has *all* the evidence, knows *all* the angles. Only *Love* understands a person's heart, their past suffering, their fears, their filters, their *stories,* and every single factor which plays into all of their choices.

Again, when Jesus was hanging on the cross, and his executioners were mocking him, he made a remarkable statement which has freed me from judging anyone. Jesus said, "Father, *forgive* them for they *know not what they do!*" Wait! What? How is that even possible? How could they have not known what they were doing? They had just hammered stakes through the hands and feet of Jesus while he screamed and writhed in pain! But in that declaration from the cross, Jesus gave us the key to *forgiveness*: we are innocent! We cannot know the full implications of our choices, and we misjudge people and situations all the time. Jesus was hung on a cross for a perceived blasphemy by the religious leaders of His day. He was condemned to death from a faulty mindset of fear and a false perception of loyalty to *God.* This is no different from the radical Muslims, or Hitler, who perceive people outside their religion as evil and believe they are serving their *God* by riding the earth of *their* perceived evil.

Parents don't set out to bruise their children's tender spirits—but they do. Our lovers don't make commitments to *Love* us, randomly abandon their promises, and wake up one day determined to destroy us—even though our lovers can sometimes be a source of great suffering.

We must understand that wounded people, which nearly all of us are, make choices from their wounds; hurt people hurt people! People who have done the work of healing their inner wounds rarely make choices that hurt themselves or others.

If we can have grace for the wounds of others and don't take anything they say or do personally if we can pause before we pass judgment, and say, "I *forgive* him/her because they don't know what they are doing," then we can avoid ever needing to let go of an offense and simply live in a state of grace. This state of grace is equally beneficial to our quality of peace and happiness, as well as it is to the wounded soul who showed up messy.

2. There are no victims: No one can take advantage of us; we must have agreed to, or said yes to, someone's request or behavior. At the very least we didn't say no or stop them from doing something we may feel was beyond our permission (except in the case of an assault by a random stranger or abuse as a child).

For this reason, I found it amazingly easy to stay in a relationship with an alcoholic binge drinker year after year without holding onto any offenses. I realized Tim wasn't choosing to hurt me intentionally; he was choosing to self-medicate. I also knew that *I* was choosing to stay in the relationship year after year for my unhealthy fear-based reasons. I was *not* a victim of Tim's choices! Both of us were doing the best we knew how to do at that time. When we know better, we make better choices, right?

3. Take Nothing Personally: If we have been offended, then *we* accepted or internally agreed with someone else's judgments, criticism, or anger and *we* chose to take it personally. In Don Miguel Ruiz's book, *The Four Agreements,* he teaches that we must recognize that what others think about us is none of our business. If we can learn to stop taking the comments, judgments, and behaviors of others personally, we can eliminate a lot of suffering in our own lives. People who judge us have a critical spirit or a negative point of view. When people act unkind or unfair toward us, it is about them being unkind and unfair; it's not about us. It's about them acting out their fears and their *stories* or childhood wounds that haven't been healed.

Consider this, My Friend: If someone accused you of being a watermelon, would you laugh or be offended? You would likely laugh, right? It is impossible for someone to offend us with a judgment we *know* is untrue. However, we might be offended if someone accuses us of something we *fear* is true or we have already judged ourselves as being true. If I think I'm stupid and someone accuses me of being stupid, I will likely become angry and try to defend my intelligence. But, if I graduated from college with the distinguished honors of Summa Cum Laude with a Ph.D. in physics and someone calls me stupid, I will just laugh that off and walk away. This is a good indicator that what you are taking personally is a *story* or a *button* that needs your undivided attention for some healing.

4. We Are All Equal: It's critical that we understand that we too are equally capable of committing the same hurtful choices given the right circumstances. True humility is the ability to recognize that we are all the same, with the same propensity for greatness, for being hurt, for making mistakes, *and* for hurting others.

Regarding this principle on *forgiveness,* I found in the Christian scriptures a story about how Jesus leveled the sinplayingfield several times—making equal the murderer and those who hate, the adulterer

106

and those who lust. At one point Jesus tells a crowd, who are getting ready to stone a woman to death for committing adultery, that anyone who was without any sin was qualified to cast the first stone. Everyone put down their stones and walked away. Why? Because, before Jesus invited them to consider their own sins, they weren't thinking about their misses, they were focused on the woman caught in adultery. That's convenient, don't you think?

Galatians 6:3 says, "Don't take this opportunity to think you are better than those who slip because you aren't: then you become the fool and deceive even yourself." MSG

Knowing that all humans get angry, all humans lust, and all humans covet what doesn't belong to them, Jesus, once again, draws a line in the sand and challenges us to cross it. If, after we examine ourselves, we find we aren't any less guilty of committing those same offenses, *then* we are free to judge. Jesus didn't make those comparisons to make people more vigilant in their pursuit of righteousness. He made those comparisons to say that all of us make poor choices sometimes, at some level, so we are all equal, and we *all* need grace!

Dear One, if you are having trouble *forgiving* someone for a perceived wrong, I invite you to consider your own misses, aka "sins." "Why do you look at the speck that is in your brother's eye but do not notice the log that is in your own eye? First, take the log out of your own eye, then you will see clearly to help your brother with the speck in his." Matthew 7:3-5

Example:

I was speaking with a client, Rob, who was appalled and quite angry after visiting a friend who was passed out drunk on the floor with a young child running around unsupervised and hungry. Now, don't get me wrong, this is child abuse, and I would have called Child Protective Services because that would have been in the best interest of both my friend and her child. Rob then went on to tell me that he didn't understand that neglectful behavior because his own daughter was, "… his whole life." However, this man has struggled with drug and alcohol abuse and has been to prison a few times for his "misses." So, without hesitation, I suggested that while I'm sure he deeply *Loves* his daughter, she wasn't, "his whole life," because his choices weren't in his child's best interest—*either.* I suggested that he was guilty of hurting his little girl as much, if not more, than the mother he was standing in self-righteous judgment over. Rob's choices to self-medicate and break the law repeatedly removed his presence from his daughter, causing her to feel abandoned. This man's daughter is now an angry young woman who doesn't ever want to see her father again.

Isn't it interesting that Rob wasn't able to see his own misses relative to his friend's? How is that possible? Because, My Friend, he was only considering the particular *situation* rather than the *impact,* or injury, on both innocent children. He didn't think he was *like* the woman he was judging because he didn't pass out, leaving his child unattended; therefore, he believed himself to be *better* than the accused.

How often does this happen in our world? We pass judgments on others without even considering if we are guilty of the same painful impact upon others. If we imagine the faces of those we feel entitled to judge as a mirror, and use their behaviors as a tool to examine ourselves carefully, we will find our own mistakes, and messy hurtful selves, staring back at us longing for *Grace* and *forgiveness.*

Living in a paradigm of *Grace* frees us to *Love* others, rather than judge them and further add to their wounds and ours. Grace is the *fruit* of a deeply self-examined life; it is the fruit of humility which recognizes that we are all equal messy human beings. "Do to others as you would have them do to you." Whom among us doesn't want to be *forgiven* for our mistakes? Whom among us doesn't have regrets and wish we could undo something that hurt another person?

My Friend, you and I currently live in a state of grace with *God*! We have been *forgiven* for all of our misses without even asking. We have done nothing to deserve *God's* beautiful gifts or *Their forgiveness*. We have done nothing to enjoy all the gifts of nature. Those gifts are available to the person who is kind and *Loving*, and to the person so blinded by their wounds that they spend their days inflicting suffering on those around them.

Matthew 10:8 admonishes, "Freely you have received; freely give." Dear Friend, deeply consider this word: *For-give. For* whom? *For* you, My Friend. *For* the world. *Give. Give* what? *Give* grace. *Give* compassion. *Give* thanks. *Give Love, My* Friend!

Love well, My Friend, and *Love* will return to you in abundance! This is the cry of your soul! This is the cry of the world! *Love* wins—but only 100 percent of the time.

I see *Forgiveness* as a two-sided coin. On one side is our need to shift our *perspectives* and investigate our *assumptions* in such a way that we are set free from the side effects of bitterness. The other side is releasing the *energy* produced by those perceived offenses that are trapped in our body. That stored negative energy leads to many of our physical diseases (dis-ease) caused by a mental state of resentment. For a deeper understanding of this principle, please visit louisehay.com for some excellent resources on physical healing and *forgiveness*.

In 2003, I attended a four-day self-awareness program called, Breakthrough Training (www.accd.org), which gave me an opportunity to release all of that pent-up negative energy that I didn't know was operating beneath my state of awareness. In the class, we were instructed to hit a pillow with open palms as fast and as hard as we could while yelling at our "offender" (which was the pillow) all the things we never got to say. For me, it was my father-wounds, which were the most painful, though I had the opportunity to address all of my painful memories. I remember shouting out my fears, anger, and deep sorrow over my father's abandonment. I mourned the loss of my father for the first time in my life at the age of 42. It took four times going through that process for me to feel emptied of all of those negative emotions which left me with a sense of peace and genuine *Love* for my father in place of pain. It was significant and critical that I was able to get all of that negative energy out of my body in that way. I know of no other way to get in touch with, and rid oneself of, those emotions thoroughly than what I experienced in that Breakthrough Training. I strongly recommend you do the same either with the support of that program or with the support of a qualified therapist.

*SECRET INGREDIENT 5 CONCEPT: *Forgiveness Is Essential for Our Healing, Happiness, and Freedom*

1. The Four Stages of Forgiveness
    1. I have to forgive
    2. I need to forgive
    3. I want to forgive
    4. There is nothing to forgive
2. Change the interpretation of the event to support *Grace* and forgiveness.

3. We are offended by the criticism of others that we already believe is true about ourselves.

4. Humility (the acceptance that we are all equal) makes forgiveness natural and effortless.

FAN THE FLAME

1. Which of the *4 Stages of Forgiveness* describes where you are right now?

2. Who do you need to forgive? Are you making any assumptions? Have you thoroughly gathered all the evidence (including asking the offender what he/she meant by their words/choices)? Are you confident you can say if it was the offender's *intention* to hurt you? You can also take your situation through the Mirror Exercises and then through the *Holy Healing* process for the best results.

3. If you feel like a victim: How did you contribute to your suffering? Did you say, "Yes"? Did you neglect to say, "No"? Did you set healthy boundaries? Did you accept the criticism or judgments of others as true? Did you take someone's choices or judgments personally?

4. In what ways is your offender a mirror for you? Of what, exactly, are you accusing someone else? What have you not been aware of in your choices or judgments that have hurt others?

5. Having done this work, are you now able to fully forgive? If not (that's OK too), I suggest you spend time with *Spirit* in stillness and ask for [*His*] mind on these matters; journal your process with *God*.

Dear God of All— In All, cleanse my mind of all false beliefs that I might experience the healing and freedom that comes from knowing the truth. Raise my awareness to my self-imposed suffering. I give my thoughts to You. Shine Your light of truth and deliver me from darkness.

And so it is, My Friend, and so it is!

THE BINDING INGREDIENTS OF "US"

Recipes need binding ingredients to hold form. A meatloaf without egg and breadcrumbs will fall apart and just be ground hamburger. A cake mix without eggs or oil will crumble. There are certain relationship behaviors that hold us together or cause us to crumble as well.

SECRET INGREDIENT 6

COMMUNICATION IS "US"

"Make every effort to keep the oneness of the Spirit in the bond of peace [each individual working together to make the whole successful]."
EPH 4:3

My Friend, a relationship is only as good as the communication skills of both partners. I believe communication is the real work of every relationship. Why do I believe this? It has been my experience with every person I have ever coached that poor communication skills are at the root of every issue in their relationship. Effective communication can be a difficult skill to master. If your relationship is struggling, I assert that poor communication is a big part of that experience. Many times we neglect to communicate our thoughts, feelings, or fears with our partner because we are afraid that discussing difficult issues will result in conflict. Or, we are afraid we will be judged as weak, ignorant, selfish, etc.

Most people make many more *assumptions* about an individual or situation rather than ask questions to *discover* what might be true for the other person. Why do we do that? Because, Dear Friend, we *assume* that the rest of the world is just like us and we know what our motives are, what our intentions are, what *we* would do, say, etc. So, we *assume* other people think, process, feel, and act like we would in that given situation. But we can't know if we are right or not unless we ask questions.

The bottom line is this: we communicate ineffectively because we haven't been taught how to communicate *well.*

What exactly is communication? According to Dictionary 2.2.1 (1994) "Communication (from Latin *communicāre*, meaning "to share") is the ***purposeful*** activity of information exchanged between two or more participants in order to convey or receive the *intended* meanings."

We are always communicating, even when we aren't saying a word. Communication is one or more of these facets: the words we use, our tone of voice, body language, silence, and listening. I will also address feedback and negotiation as useful forms of communication in this section.

LISTENING

My Friend, I don't know if we could be any worse at the skill of listening than if we were born deaf! In our society, people are trained to talk *at* others rather than *with* others. We seem to be so wrapped up in being right, and defending ourselves, that we completely miss the hearts of our lovers. Even if your partner is coming from a wounded and fearful place, using those deadly control behaviors I taught you about in Secret Ingredient 3. If you are fully present and listening *to* those complaints through the filter of *Love*, and *if* you can detach what your partner is saying from a personal attack, you will be able to fully support your lover and deepen your relationship.

Listening is actually a skill of *focused attention* and being completely present without an agenda. What do I mean by *focused attention*? I mean that the only goal you have when listening to your lover is to fully understand *them*, not so much understand their position or opinions—although that is important, too. More importantly, you need to understand *him/her* as a person. What are your lover's fears, frustrations, values, longings, hopes, dreams, or disappointments? What have they given up on? What holds them back from pursuing their dreams? What drives them? What gets them out of bed in the morning full of anticipation and passion? What keeps them in bed in the morning afraid of what the day may hold? What's missing for them in their relationship with you or others? What needs to be healed in them to truly make them happy?

When we *listen* with an agenda to be right or to fix something, we can totally miss what our lovers are actually saying. Most people aren't really *listening to* their mate they are formulating a response or defense to the first sentence or so of the conversation.

Example:

I will never forget a beautiful story about a young adult man who was a Bible theologian raised by an atheist father. The son spent his adult life debating the gospel with foreign dignitaries and scholars of other religions. After about 10 years of his career, he decided to enroll his father into his work by asking him if he would share his position on atheism. The son told his father that he greatly respected him, and valued his intellect. The son told his father he knew he had done a lot of research on the subject of *God,* and based on what he discovered, he conclude there was no *God*. The son honored his father's intelligence and his research, as well as his choices. The son believed that by inviting his father to present his best findings against his own belief in *God,* he would gain great insight, and it would equip him to better understand his father as well as better address the same arguments around the world. This son actually *listened* to understand his father's position, not to be right about his own beliefs. This kind of active *listening* is a beautiful gift to give to anyone we *Love*—even to a stranger.

I have had countless conversations with numerous friends, family members, and acquaintances. I can tell you from all of those experiences that people miss each other by not asking questions. When you think about it, there are an infinity of questions we could ask people; but we rarely do. Joe and I *Love* to ask questions—possibly to a fault. It is shocking to us how few people ever ask us questions even after having spent hours responding to our questions. It just doesn't occur to them to discover something more about us. We don't take that personally either.

Example:

Have you ever spent time with someone who is excellent at asking questions? I will never forget the *first* time this happened for me: it was with Joe. On our first unofficial date, Joe and I sat in a bar for three hours while he asked me question after question about my life, my children, my failed marriage, my friends, and my career. We were interrupted many times by a very sweet and lonely drunk man who didn't detour Joe one bit from picking up the conversation right where we left off. Never in my life did I feel more known. I remember thinking, "This must be what it's like to be on the other side of a conversation with me." In all of my relationships, I did the asking and the majority of the listening. I genuinely want to know people, and I want them to feel valuable and understood, so I ask a bunch of questions. I *give* that which I desire to receive. "Do unto others as you would have them do unto you." Remember, My Friend, the purest purpose in any relationship is to *give* rather than to *get*.

Answering questions was a new experience for me, but I felt safe to pour out my life in front of this stranger. I felt safe because this man really wanted to understand me. I didn't sense any agenda with him, just a sincere, compassionate man who was available to listen. No one had ever asked me the questions Joe was asking. After those three hours, Joe knew things about me that my ex-husband and closest friends didn't know, only because he asked questions and they didn't.

One of the beautiful fruits of someone asking you questions is the opportunity to get very clear about things that are only left in your head. Having conversations out loud *sounds* different. We get to *hear* ourselves talk; the result is that we can discover something new about ourselves in the process.

I believe we all long to be known. It creates value for us when someone shows an interest in our beliefs, thoughts, hopes, disappointments, and fears. Most people won't just offer up information like that. Instead, many engage in shallow and meaningless conversations about the weather, where we bought our shoes, sports, or gossip. Ever leave a gathering having spent hours talking about nothing significant and feel like your life energy was sucked out of you, and you just wasted those hours of your life? Ever leave a friend or group of friends where there was a deep, meaningful, stimulating, inspiring conversation? Those conversations are synergistic, inspiring, energizing, resourceful, and compelling. Joe and I are addicted to those kinds of conversations; we attempt to have deeper conversations with nearly everyone we meet.

I find it quite surprising and honoring how quickly people will share intimate things with me, a virtual stranger. I believe it's because people are hurting in secret. They are alone in their deepest fears and struggles because no one is being sensitive to their depressed energy, or asking them questions. Perhaps they don't feel safe enough to share with their families and friends for fear of being judged.

Example:

Recently, Joe and I had a dear friend over who is fearless when it comes to sharing her heart wide open with us. We spent two hours talking about her struggles and victories. Joe and I asked her a lot of questions, which she seemed grateful to answer. We noticed her energy shift from anxiety to a calmness, because she was able to empty her emotional basket as we delved deeper into her fears by asking questions. One of the beautiful gifts of probing fears with questions is it exposes those fears for what they are—lies. Once those fears are illuminated, we can see how unfounded they are, and we can easily replace them with a *truth* that supports peace and joy in our lives. Most of us need someone else to help us process through those fears. This is where a loving partner, who can ask great questions, is very supportive. Or, you can always hire me to process your fears and frustrations.

Whenever I notice Joe's energy has diminished from his typical "sunshine" to melancholy, I *always* check in with him by asking, "Honey, what's going on with you? I notice a decline in your energy." That question leads into a conversation about something Joe is struggling with, which is almost always about some future fear that hasn't happened yet. As he is able to talk it all the way through, he can get a different perspective on the situation, and his peace is quickly restored. Those conversations wouldn't happen if I were not aware enough to discern his energy and ask him questions, instead of making an assumption.

My Friend, please notice that I'm talking about *asking questions* not about giving advice. It's vital that you learn to ask, then listen, then ask again. Being a great listener is a beautiful gift for others. As we are fully present with our lover, and they are sharing their fears and frustrations, we can *listen* for their deepest fears and ask more questions to better support them.

Example:

Tony and I were talking about a situation regarding his daughter, Helen. Tony told me he wanted to call Helen's boyfriend and chastise him for being inconsiderate to her. When I asked him what *his fear* was, he paused and said, "That's an excellent question. I didn't know I was afraid of anything, but now that you ask, I'm afraid she will be hurt in that relationship if her boyfriend isn't more considerate towards her."

"Uh-huh," I said. "And, if Helen gets hurt, then what? Do you believe that Helen is capable of surviving hurt feelings, or is she really fragile? Do you believe that Helen is healthy enough to set good boundaries with others? Do you think Helen can learn something valuable from this experience with her boyfriend?"

"She is a strong young woman, really strong! I'm not sure about healthy boundaries, but I do think she can learn something from this experience," Tony said.

I then asked, "Do you think getting involved will communicate to her that you think she is strong or fragile?"

"Fragile," he said.

"Is that what you want for her?" I asked.

"No!" he said.

"What do you think would better support her then?" I asked.

"I think I'll suggest that Helen takes a close look at the way her boyfriend treats her and ask her some questions about their relationship to see if there is anything *she* wants to change," he replied.

Do you see, My Friend, how I just kept asking more questions to help *Tony* discover something better than rescuing his daughter from a minor issue, which wasn't his business anyway.

OBSTACLES TO EFFECTIVE LISTENING:

- Formulating a response while the other person is still speaking

- Interrupting your partner

- Neglecting to further investigate your partner's concerns by asking more questions

- Allowing your mind to wander while your partner is still sharing

- Judging your partner's delivery, message, outfit, etc.

- Giving advice without being asked to do so

- **Defending yourself – Don't do it, ever!**

EFFECTIVE LISTENING TOOLS:

- Maintain eye contact; never look at something or someone else.

- Give focused and full attention to the person speaking. Your phone should be in another room or Airplane Mode. Unless you are waiting for an emergency call or the birth of a baby, there really isn't a good enough reason to check every text or call immediately. It speaks value to your lover, friend, or family when you set aside time to be with just them, especially for these deeper conversations.

- Periodically check in to be sure you are clear about your partner's message by asking, "Let me see if I understand you correctly," then share what you heard. Then ask, "Did I hear you right? Is this what you're saying?"

- If they answer, "No," ask them to tell you again or to clarify their point. Listen again carefully without any filters.

- If, at any time, you aren't tracking with your partner, let them know that you don't understand and ask them to repeat what they said.

- When your partner seems to be finished, ask, "Is there anything else you would like to share about _____?"

- Lastly, ask, "How do you feel about this issue?" if they haven't already discussed their feelings.

- Share with your lover what you understood them to have said and especially how they are feeling about the topic so they feel heard and known. Try to relate what your partner shared with you with a past experience of the same situation. Doing that is also helpful in communicating that you understand their problem/concern/fear/disappointment; just don't hijack the conversation. Once you've shared a connecting story, return to where they left off and ask another question.

- Finish by thanking them for trusting you enough to share their heart with you.

- You may want to take some time to consider your partner's conversation before you respond.

- DO NOT DEFEND YOURSELF, EVER!

Example:

Cyndi is a dear, close friend of mine. Due to her own personal issues, she decided to withdraw from our friendship after my divorce. Over the course of the following two years, we had a few surface conversations but nothing profound, and certainly nothing like the connection we had before my divorce. After one brief conversation on the phone regarding a personal issue, I was able to support her in a way that I believe reminded her of my *Love* for her, and that I was her trusted friend. A few weeks later, she came over for a visit. She opened up and shared about her struggles with a relationship that wasn't going well. I listened carefully to her and asked many questions to help her discover for herself her deepest fears. I confirmed her disappointments and fears by sharing with her stories from my past that were very similar to hers. There was a deep and instant connection because she felt heard and understood since I had strikingly similar struggles in my past. I didn't try to fix her or give her any of the tools I'm teaching in this book; I listened, asked clarifying questions, and shared stories that supported her.

Since that conversation, our relationship has been restored to the same close, fun, *Loving* experience we enjoyed and treasured for years prior to my divorce. I still don't know why there was a pause in our relationship on her part, even after asking questions about what happened for her. What is important is that our relationship is restored. I believe that connecting with Cyndi through listening, asking questions, and sharing similar stories reunited our hearts as friends. This is the power of listening to understand, not to be right.

BODY LANGUAGE

Studies show that people are much more likely to believe someone's body language if a person's physical communication conflicts with their words. If you ask me how I'm feeling, and I say, "I'm fine," but my eyes are cast down, my energy is obviously low, and my mouth is turned downward in a frown, you will likely interpret my physical response as suffering rather than "fine."

Example:

Shortly after serving on a self-realization team, I decided to address an issue with my husband, Tim, that was brought to the surface during that experience. I asked Tim if we could talk about something that I learned about *myself*. Tim was sitting on the couch, leaning forward with his elbows on his knees facing me, and looking in my eyes. Tim's body language communicated he was open to hearing what I had to say as well as interested. From what I could see, I had Tim's full attention.

I told him that I realized how much I was starving for affirmation from *him*. While I was on the self-realization team, I was being affirmed for my thoughtful service, my attention to details, the way I *Love* people, and on my appearance. What I noticed was that every time someone else affirmed me, my heart longed to hear those things from Tim. Tim was the object of my affection, and it was *his* approval I longed for most. What happened next was so revealing it was as if Tim was shouting at me with his body language, "Stop talking, I can't handle this conversation!" Tim immediately sat back into the couch, crossed his arms over his chest [protecting his heart], crossed his leg, and put his hands in his lap [protecting his "manhood" from being emasculated]. He immediately shut down! What Tim "said" with his body language was loud and clear.

Noticing his body language, I pressed in to understand I then asked Tim, "Honey, what just happened? What did you hear me say?" To which he responded, "I'm a terrible husband, a terrible father, and I'm never going to get this right." What Tim revealed to me was his limited capacity to hear that he wasn't perfect. That response wasn't because of what I said, it was the result of Tim's internal critic who was constantly judging and criticizing *him*. Tim held so much judgement of himself, there wasn't room for one more thing, i.e. my conversation about my longing for affirmations from him.

After Tim had responded to my question, I told him that it wasn't my intention to make him feel attacked. I pointed out to him that I wasn't referring to him as an overall person, father, or husband. I only wanted him to know how important his approval and affirmations were for *me*. Unfortunately, Tim couldn't hear that either because of his own self-judgments.

Scripture teaches that if our sight (perspective) is dark (negative, critical, judgmental), then we will only be able to see darkness in ourselves, in others, and in our circumstances. If our sight (perspective) is light (positive, encouraging, accepting, and *Loving*), then we will see light everywhere in everyone.

I realized in an instant that Tim didn't have the capacity to hear my needs without crashing. His response made sharing with Tim unsafe; I felt bad and wrong for even having any needs. After all, I had gone 24 years without being affirmed in the ways that would have meant the most to me; I could go without his verbal affirmation a lot longer. The result: he shut down and I shut down—another step back, away from each other.

My Friend, if you can learn not to take things your lover says or does personally (like Tim did in the above example), there will be much more freedom and appreciation for both of you to share your desires, your frustrations, and your fears with each other. Staying *neutral* during any conversation will result in drawing you together and deepening your trust and passion for each other.

The reason I chose this story to share with you, My Friend, is to highlight the effects of "listening" intently to body language. There have been many occasions I have been able to support clients just by watching their body language and discerning their energy. Body language and energy are forms of *feedback*. They communicate a person's response to someone else, or circumstances that they either are happy or unhappy about.

Example:

Louise was an elderly client who came to see me because she was severely depressed. Louise spent her life performing for the approval of others since she was a small child. Her husband had been critical of her disposition to worry. If Louise didn't have a smile on her face, her husband would reprimand and shame her; so, she learned to train her facial muscles to be in a constant state of a smile. Have you ever seen someone fake a smile? It looks, well, fake! Louise was sharing a painful story with me one day with this permanent fake smile distorting her face, which was totally incongruent with her troubling story. When I asked her how she was feeling, she said, "My heart is broken." To which I replied, "You need to tell your face." My intention was to help her to connect with those around her whom she deeply *Loved* by being authentic— by being sure that her words and body language were congruent. How would anyone know how much this woman was hurting with a frozen smile on her face? That "smile" communicated so much fear, insecurity, and bondage to me. Because of my ability to "hear" body language, I was able to break through her years of performing, and helped her become more authentic regardless of her husband's criticism.

Example:

In a couples coaching session with Ryan and Lori, I noticed that both of them were displaying resistance through their body language. Resistance is often a response to a *perceived* attack. Notice I said, "perceived attack." This is because unless, and until, a comment is investigated by the listener, they can only guess at their partner's intention and make an assumption. More often than not, a comment just pushes a *button*. Whose problem is *your* button? Yours, right? Whose problem is your *lover's* button? Theirs, right? These two had no clue that they were perfectly mirroring each other's behavior and judgments. Both of them wanted to be heard, but neither of them were interested in listening to the other in an open and non-resistant way; neither were *giving* what they longed for in the relationship.

Ryan and Lori were sitting next to each other on a couch. Neither of them made eye contact with the other. Ryan started talking to the ceiling at one point, while Lori sank further and further into the couch, hanging her head in the position of shame and defeat. What I discerned from Ryan's body language was that as he was literally talking into thin air—a physical posture of feeling unheard. Lori's body language told me she felt defeated and was giving up—a physical posture of believing you are not enough or can't do something right. If you aren't even looking at your lover during a conversation, how will you know that there is something critical going on beneath their words? Asking questions could open up greater intimacy and possibilities for both of them.

While many people will pick up on someone's body language, what they do next is the most critical to the conversation. More often than not, we will notice something, and then make an assumption about the meaning of what we saw or heard, rather than ask questions to find out what someone meant by their statement, complaint, or behavior.

When I investigated the signals of Ryan and Lori's body language, they discovered that neither of them felt heard or understood. Both of them did a lot of talking, but no one was listening. Ryan and Lori were dying in a relationship with a faulty foundation of *getting*. Teaching this couple to *give* to the other that which they longed to receive themselves turned this relationship around.

I believe the eyes are the window to our souls. Making eye contact is so telling of both the speaker and the listener. Eye contact is a form of body language that says, "You have my full attention," from the listener and, "I feel safe enough to share my heart with you," from the speaker. Avoiding eye contact says, "I feel insecure sharing this with you," from the speaker and, "I'm not fully present," from the listener.

My Friend, it is both *Loving* and respectful to look someone in the eye when in a conversation. Put down your cell phone, turn off the TV, and turn off your computer when your lover (or anyone) has something to share with you. We can even tune into whether someone is multitasking while we are talking on the phone with them. If I become aware that I don't have Joe's full attention while we are talking on the phone, I will ask him if he's busy and tell him I will call him back if he doesn't have time right now for the call. It's impossible to actually listen well while doing something else. If we are busy and don't have time to give someone our full attention, we should say so and schedule a *talktime*. If we sense that someone isn't listening, we should simply acknowledge that, without getting offended (don't take anything personally), and ask them for a better time to chat.

TONE

There are some conflicting statistics regarding the percentages of communication forms, so I'm not going to cite any here. Suffice it to say, body language and tone speak louder than words. If I say, "I forgive you" in a flippant tone without compassion, you will likely interpret that as insincere or me trying to avoid a more vulnerable conversation and trying to avoid the truth of how I actually feel.

Have you ever had an email or text taken completely wrong? Ever wonder how in the world someone interpreted a message you sent that couldn't be further from your intention? It's because written words have no body language or tone. It's literally up to the receiver to discern your words, and most people will do that through their own filters without any indicators as to your real meaning. Those personal filters can be one of shame, fear, insecurity, disappointment, frustration, powerlessness. You can become the innocent recipient of someone else's past wounds. This is why it is essential that you NEVER have a serious conversation with anyone via written word. Body language and tone are responsible for a huge part of the conversation. I can say, "Are you serious?" from anger, from compassion, or from sarcasm. There is no way for you to know my intention without tone. If something lands on you negatively from a text or email, I suggest you pick up the phone and investigate the message. Make no assumptions either way—just call and ask questions so you don't take offense where none was intended. Even if an offense was intended, don't receive it. That's just an unhealed wound crying out for *Love.*

Our tone reflects our judgments. If we think we are hiding our judgments of someone, we are delusional. We can *feel* what others are thinking. And we can definitely *hear* the judgmental energy behind the often masked words through the tone those words are expressed. If we are angry and cynical, our words will be soaked in that energy regardless of how beautiful and seemingly kind the words we use.

I had a client go through the exercises at the end of this chapter. She asked her husband which of the communication forms he would like her to change. He said, "I'd love it if you changed your tone with me." My client said, "I need to work on changing my tone." I reminded her that her tone was just a reflection of her judgments. It's her *judgments* which need to change; her tone will follow without effort.

WORDS

Most people don't pay close attention to the actual words people use when communicating. Our vocabulary is powerful! Words can create or destroy, facilitate life or bring death, unite or divide countries, races, religions. Harsh words spoken to a tender child can haunt him/her and govern them his/her whole life. The words *stupid, fat,* and *ugly* have significantly wounded many lives.

Cuss words are quite powerful to express intense feelings of anger and passion. Cuss words are neutral, not evil or offensive in my opinion; they are merely a tool people reach for when nothing else seems to be working. Whenever a client uses profanity to express a strong feeling with their partner, I take notice quickly that they are asking for attention about their issue and they aren't feeling heard, or they have strong emotions, which haven't been released from their body. I use profanity whenever I believe it will get my message across more effectively than if I used a more benign word. Notice I did not say that I raise my voice or am angry. If I use profanity in a conversation, it is because I believe it will make my point as passionately as possible.

My Friend, I strongly recommend that you never take offense if your lover uses profanity; it's only a tool, no more than any other word except there is more passion attached to it. Again, don't take anything personally. Let me mention a distinction about using profanity to express strong emotions and using profanity to insult someone with name calling. Profanity is about strong emotions finding a voice, whereas name calling is a verbal attack on the other person with the intent to hurt them. Name calling is verbal abuse and shouldn't be tolerated. Still, don't take name calling personally either. Someone else's anger isn't about you, Dear Friendit's always about them.

I encourage you to pay close attention to the vocabulary your lover is using when talking with you. Notice if the words infer that they view themselves as a victim like the words, "always" and "never." Statements like, "You made me feel," or "He made me do…," or "I had to…," are all victim conversations. Whenever I hear those words, I ask questions about their situation to help them see they have simply given their power away and can have it back whenever they choose. I am passionate about empowering people. I want others to step into their own power, to control their own lives, to have the results they long for. Giving people a new language of empowerment supports them to accept their power and have different results.

FEEDBACK

Feedback comes in many forms, and I assert that it is NEVER negative! This is what I want you to understand clearly: All feedback is positive feedback. Even the worst possible feedback you could receive has the potential to greatly benefit you. Getting fired from a job because you were frequently late is positive feedback. It's an opportunity to take your business hours more seriously at the next job. Getting diabetes from abusing your body with carbs is positive feedback. It's an opportunity to change your eating habits so you don't further injure yourself with food. If your lover leaves you for another, that is positive feedback. It's an opportunity to take a close look at how you can improve your relationship skills so you can have better results in your next relationship. Or, it's an opportunity to recognize that water seeks its own level, and the two of you were no longer a good fit.

If you are engaging with someone with a lofty, arrogant attitude, and someone gives you feedback that you came across arrogant, would that be negative or positive feedback? Well, if you really are being arrogant and don't realize it, that feedback would give you an opportunity to investigate where your superior mindset or insecurity (often disguised as arrogance) comes from so you can have a different impact on others.

What I recommend is that you "try on" all feedback. What I mean by "try on" is to pause for a moment and consider if you have ever heard that feedback before. If you have heard it before, it is likely true. You can then decide how you want to shift your behavior or your approach to have the results you prefer. If the feedback you received was off the wall and no one else had ever told you that before, or, when you heard the feedback there wasn't a check in your *Spirit* that it was true, you can then dismiss it as the other person's filters misdirecting their perspective. If the feedback lands on you with a sting, it's likely true, and you know it, even if you are resisting the feedback at the time.

I encourage all of my clients to get comfortable with feedback—to welcome it as a friend rather than resist it as an enemy.

I *Love* feedback! I sent the manuscript of this book to several friends, many times, to get their feedback so I could offer the best product to you as possible. I received my friends' feedback as a gift from them, as *Loving* support, even when I was disappointed at what they suggested that I remove, or where they told me I needed to add clarity to a concept. Then, I got to investigate any *emotional buttons* that got triggered in me from their feedback, which lead to more self-discovery, more healing, more empowerment, and one more step towards wholeness. Do you see, My Friend, how feedback is such a great gift?

Example:

When Joe and I were getting ready to move into our RV to travel America, I had to get rid of three-fourths of my clothes. I enlisted Joe's support with that process by giving him a fashion show. I asked him to just give a thumbs up or down to let me know what he liked and didn't. Joe's feedback made choosing what to keep and toss very fast and simple. I decided that what mattered most to me was whether or not *he* liked what I was wearing. I loved all of my clothes, but I could only keep a few. I kept the clothes Joe loved on me the most. That was a win-win for me! Now I know that whatever I wear Joe likes on me as well.

The *Universe* gives us feedback as well, only it's not biased! This is called Karma, or sowing and reaping. We can actually look at the current circumstances of our lives and know that those results are feedback of *our* own thoughts and choices. This is powerful to understand. Most people don't recognize this truth so they keep doing the same things over and over, expecting different results. They don't realize that the results they have are always going to be the same unless they think better thoughts and make better choices. This is a natural law. These are *Universal* laws that apply to everyone everywhere. *Universal* feedback doesn't change because we are white or black or Jewish or Muslim. These *Universal Laws,* which govern the Earth, are just like gravity; they are always working, whether we are aware of them or not, believe in them or not, and agree with them or not! You can argue with gravity, but you will lose 100 percent of the time! Same is true of the *Law of Attraction,* Karma, and sowing and reaping!

Universal feedback is consistent for everyone, for every action, for every mindset. I know a young woman who is homeless by her choices. She often steals from stores without getting caught. Other homeless people who use drugs and alcohol steal from her to support their habits. That is *Universal* feedback; that is Karma. Just because she isn't getting caught by the department stores and put in jail, doesn't mean she is getting away with anything.

If all you do is talk about how terrible your life is, or how you are a victim and powerless, the feedback you will receive for that mindset is a life of suffering and constantly being taken advantage of. If you are lazy and don't want to work, your feedback will be one of lack. If you are a workaholic and never rest your body, your feedback will be physical illness. I know of a young woman who is terrified to make choices for her own life because it will upset her father. The feedback her body is giving her for performing rather than being authentic, for trying to keep peace with her father, is war in her body; this girl is getting so sick, soon she will be too ill to perform any longer.

My Friend, feedback can serve you well in this life. I recommend you become very comfortable receiving and recognizing all forms of feedback to get the most out of this gift. Remember, Dear One, what we resist persists, and that's just a lot of unnecessary suffering from my perspective.

NEGOTIATION

The innate nature of a *Loving* relationship is to please our partner. Problems arise when the differences in the way we approach life don't fit perfectly into our ideal image of a romantic relationship. What happens when we want our partner to change a behavior, but they aren't willing to change? How do we navigate through a relationship with someone who does life so differently, and more likely *wrong* from our perspective? Negotiation.

Negotiation works like this: I bring my request to the table for discussion, and *you* decide what *you* are willing to do to move towards my request. There is no arguing or defending. There is no performing, and there are no victims. There is simply making a request and allowing your partner to choose to change or not—a little or a lot. The only alternative is to engage in controlling behaviors, which we already know don't work!

We must accept the fact that each of us approaches life differently, and we have different needs, likes, dislikes, and wants. Remember, the purpose of these romantic relationships is not to conform someone into some ideal image we hold in our minds about how our partner *should* be. For these relationships to remain passionate and truly *loving,* we must practice *allowing without resistance.* If, after making a request, your partner doesn't offer a compromise and doesn't want to change, you have two options. Let go of the possibility of having what you want, without any resentment, or leave the relationship if it's a deal-breaker for you.

A word of caution: If you insist on getting what you want, and tell your lover that you will end the relationship if he/she doesn't change—you'd better mean it! Make sure you would rather live without this person, and all the other beautiful attributes and gifts they bring to your world, before you give them that ultimatum. This fear-based strategy blew up in a client's face. Maria thought her husband would change some of his behaviors if he knew how serious she was by telling him she wanted him to move out if he didn't change. This man said he was relatively happy in his marriage and never would have left his wife until he was out on his own for a few months and realized how heavy his wife's expectations and controlling behaviors had been on him. After a few months of freedom, Maria's husband chose to end their marriage. Had Maria known then what she found out later, she never would have threatened her husband with the ultimatum, "change or divorce"—because Maria never wanted a divorce.

Example:

Janet and John came to see me because of a recurring argument they couldn't seem to resolve. John worked evenings, five days a week. Janet complained on a regular basis about his night shift. She kept telling John to quit his job and get another one so she and their kids could spend more time with him. John was on the ground floor of a business opportunity and saw a great future with the company. John was considering both his financial future as well as being able to spend more time with his family as he was promoted within the organization. I asked Janet what was the minimum John could do to satisfy her needs and support their relationship. Thinking for a moment, Janet asked if John could be home two hours earlier two nights a week to spend with the family. John was shocked that she asked for so little time, given all the arguments they had over his current schedule. When I asked John if he could accommodate her request, he said he could be home two hours earlier *three* nights a week if he went in on Saturday morning for four hours. Janet was elated, and John was happy to find a way to please his wife and stay the course with his career. Interesting that neither of them considered a compromise for all of the conversations/arguments they had about this issue.

What I've noticed about the art of negotiation is that it's quite simple, but often overlooked. It seems we are programmed for *all or nothing* options, rather than *compromise* solutions. In the example above, neither John or Janet considered less than what they each wanted. They thought the only option was *all or nothing at all.* Keep this in mind the next time you have a difference with your lover.

We need to be sure we are *effectively* communicating *Love* and support to our partners. We need to be open to coming together to negotiate a compromise for *our* relationships. If you think about it carefully, there really are three entities within every relationship. There is "You" and your needs, "Me" and my needs, and "Us" and our needs. We do the best if we run all of our choices and conversations through the filter of "Us" first. It would be powerful to ask yourself the question, "Is what I'm about to do or say going to support my lover *and our* relationship or tear it down?" None of our choices are neutral. Every one of them either supports "Us" or separates "Us." We must learn to make more conscious choices through the filter of "Us" if we are going to experience a *Real Passion Revolution* with our lovers.

CONCLUSION

My Friend, I have been around a while! I have been a student of human behavior for a very long time. I have no idea *why* we aren't better at communicating after hundreds of thousands of years doing so, but we aren't! Most people actually suck at this fundamental relationship skill. It's no wonder so many relationships don't work out. Learn the beautiful gift of listening and asking questions without taking anything personally. Learn to discern body language, ask more questions, ask for feedback from your lover, and listen to *Universal* feedback. Learn the skill of negotiation with your lover so you can both benefit from having your needs fulfilled. My Friend, if you want to experience *Real Passion Revolution* with your lover, then become an effective communicator!

An interesting, beautiful, and unexpected side effect of never using controlling or critical behaviors in my relationship with Joe is that he is more than happy to support me in every way, with or without my requests. I realized just how powerful this sowing and reaping was when I fully put it into action. *Give* to your lover that which you desire to receive, and your lover will give in return. If you desire him/her to listen to you and to understand you, listen to and try to understand him/her. If you want to be able to have any conversation with your lover without him/her getting upset, be a safe place for him/her to share whatever is on his/her heart. For those of you who have done damage to your relationship, it will take a while to reap a new harvest with your lover, but your relationship will change if you stay focused on *only* sowing *Loving,* supportive, empowering behaviors with your lover. Do not allow one more destructive word or behavior into your relationship; you will experience a *Real Passion Revolution* of your own.

*SECRET INGREDIENT 6 CONCEPT: *Effective Communication Tools*

1. Active Listening
2. Obstacles to Effective Listening
3. Effective Listening Skills
4. Body Language
5. Tone
6. Words
7. Feedback
8. Negotiation

FAN THE FLAME

1. Give yourself a score of 1 – 10 for each of the 6 components of effective communication: 1. *Listening* 2. *Body Language* 3. *Tone* 4. *Words* 5. *Feedback* 6. *Negotiation*

2. Of the 6 communication components, which do you think you need to work on the most? Which do you believe you do well?

3. Share your perceptions of yourself with your lover and ask him/her to rate you as well. Be sure you ask them to be completely honest with their answers. Reassure them they will not be in trouble if they give you a low number for any or all components. Remember, whatever they say is true for them and is *positive* feedback for you. If you believe yourself to be an excellent communicator, but your lover gives you a 3 in every communication component, that only means that there is room for improvement. **Never defend yourself!**

4. Ask your lover what you can do to bring each of the 6 communication components to a 10 for them.

5. If the current condition of your relationship is merely feedback for what you have been sowing into it, what do you now see you have been doing/saying that isn't working to produce the *Loving* relationship that you desire?

6. What do you now see you must *give* to your partner to have what you long for?

Dear God of All— In All, I am listening to understand all that I can as I'm reading this material. Raise my awareness to listen and communicate effectively so my lover feels heard and known. Open my ears and my eyes wide enough to take in all of the verbal and nonverbal communication cues so I can hear the spoken words, and the unspoken, that are being shared. Teach me to hear what You hear, and see what You see, so I might understand in the deepest and most profound ways—so that I can Love as You Love.

And so it is, My Friend, and so it is!

SECRET INGREDIENT 7

FREEDOM [*LOVE*] BINDS "US"

"Christ has set us free to live a free life. So take your stand!
Never again let anyone put a harness of slavery on you."
Gal 5:1 MSG

From birth, we crave *freedom*; we want what we want, and we want it when we want it! We begin to recognize that by complaining (i.e. crying) we will get picked up, fed, our diaper changed, and entertained.

Just observe a two-year-old being restrained from what he/she wants to do. The "Terrible Two's" is the season of a child's life where they are uninhibited in vocalizing their deep desire for absolute *freedom* from restrictions on their choices. This is also the time when they *learn* that they don't have the *freedom* to do as they please (Of course not, they would hurt themselves or worse)! So, as parents, we train them, day after day, that they are subject to our power over them.

In a healthy home, the older children get, the more they are given *freedom* and personal responsibility to make their own choices. The more *freedom* a parent gives their child as they mature, the more the child learns for *themselves* what works and what doesn't in life. Parents who try to maintain too much control over a child's choices will usually be met with great resistance and likely rebellion. Restrict a child too much, for too long, and they will bolt in the complete opposite direction, regardless of their own suffering by their choice to do so.

Well, guess what, My Friend? It appears that this deep longing for *freedom* isn't limited to our childhood. Try to impose restrictions on an adult, and they will eventually revolt too.

Freedom is the power to act, speak, or think as one wants without hindrance or restraint. It is a state of independence, the ability to self-govern one's life. In my opinion, *freedom* is synonymous with *Love*. *Love* never restrains another from their right to choose how they want to live their life, regardless of whether or not those choices are harmful to themselves (with the exception of a child).

CONTROL

Dear One, I really want you to understand what I am teaching here because this is a key that will unlock your own personal desires for *freedom*. This *freedom* is a pillar of strength in your special relationship with your lover. Nothing chokes the life out of a relationship faster than attempting to control one another.

The word "control" comes from the Latin root word "contra" which means *against*. No surprise then that trying to control someone is acting *against* them and *against* your relationship.

Aside from controlling our own lives and directing our children, I assert that <u>control is the fruit of an unexamined fear.</u> READ that again! We want to feel like we have some form of control in this world so we can protect ourselves and others from pain and suffering. However, control is an illusion except for the power to control only yourself—your choices, your thoughts, and your emotions. Any attempt to control another person will only result in more pain and suffering for both parties.

Wait? What? At this point, you might be filled with fear at the thought that you don't have any control of your world and the people in it. This is where I would like to invite you to trust; trust the *Universe*, trust *God*, and trust your *Intuition*. Our fears are never what they appear to be on the surface. So dig deeper, My Friend, as I taught you with the *Holy Healing* process.

Example:

When my oldest son, Jonathan, was a soldier stationed in Iraq, I was tempted to live in a constant state of fear: "What if he dies?" fear. What's that about anyway? What is my real fear? That my child will die or whether or not I would ever be happy again if my son died? Would the pain be such that it would suffocate me? How would I ever be able to have a life without my son?

What I decided to do was live each day as if my son were alive (because he was, and is alive). I would trust myself and my *God* with my future. If Jonathan were killed at war, I would suffer the loss of my precious son, but nothing could separate me from him entirely. I believe Jonathan would be with me always in *Spirit*! I lost my brother and my father, so I know what that kind of pain is like. I reminded myself that should my son not come home from war, it would be painful, but I would find my way through that pain. I was able to take my very worst fear and dismantle it, rendering it powerless in my mind and in my body, and I never suffered again from that thought. I am happy to report that Jonathan finished his military commitment and is working in the field of his passion.

I believe that worry and control are attempts to minimize the pain of loss. What we end up doing is experiencing the emotional pain of losing someone or something while we still have them/it and could be enjoying them/it. All of us will experience loss at some point in our journey here, but why in the world would we impose those painful thoughts and emotions on ourselves when in reality we haven't actually lost anything yet? The result of worry is that we end up suffering more, not less. And much of the time, the loss never comes—as in the case of my son, Jonathan. Mark Twain said it perfectly, "I am an old man and have known a great many troubles, but most of them never happened." Many of our worries will never manifest. But our brain and body feel the full impact as if they did happen because our worry actually causes the emotional pain associated with that loss.

Now, Darling, what is it that you fear the most? Which fears are driving you to attempt to control your lover? Whenever your peace is disturbed, I want you to ask yourself, "What am I afraid of?."

How exactly do we attempt to control others? According to Dr. Glasser, in *Choice Theory*, we attempt to control others by what he calls *The 7 Deadly Behaviors*: *(1) Complaining (2) Blaming (3) Nagging (4) Criticizing (5) Threatening (6) Punishing (silent treatment, withdrawal, withholding sex, doing the opposite of your partners wishes, etc.) (7) Rewarding to control (sex, money, doing what your partner wishes, etc.)*

Please keep in mind that withdrawing to process your *buttons* and withdrawing to punish are very different actions. Both you and your lover will immediately know which agenda is driving the action you are taking. Remember, we are always experiencing one another's energy and judgments whether we realize it or not!

We are also quite clear when someone is trying to control us. We instantly resist being controlled. Sometimes we aren't sure why we are resisting someone, and we don't always consciously recognize the control tactics of others, but we are clear that something feels wrong or uncomfortable in the relationship. I invite you to observe the look on a partner's face when their significant other is telling them what to do or not to do. It's often intense, and it shows all over their face!

As I mentioned earlier, it is entirely inappropriate and even arrogant to attempt to correct or control another adult. My Friend, if you engage in any of the above control behaviors I ask you to consider this, "What makes you think that you know better than the person you are attempting to control what is in his/her best interest?" Perhaps, the suffering your lover might experience by continuing along a particular path, via their poor choice, is exactly what *they* require to grow and be empowered. We must stop acting like amateur providences in the lives of others if we are going to have safe, passionate, *Loving*, fulfilling relationships with one another!

FREEDOM

This process I'm writing about here is not easy! It is simple to understand, but breaking away from control to *freedom* is a process you will likely have to practice over and over and over before it takes root. Allowing others to make their own choices without *any* resistance or assistance from you will take time and experience. I encourage you to share what you are learning with your lover and ask her/him for their support in helping you implement these tools into your relationship. It would be powerful to ask your lover about which ways they experience you trying to control them and how that feels for them.

There have been many times I have had to bite my tongue to keep from controlling Joe because I was very uncomfortable with what he was doing or saying. However, because I have been practicing these concepts for a while with amazing results, I have been able to navigate *my fears* without hurting Joe or our relationship.

Example:

When Joe and I began driving around America in our new "home" (RV), we had little experience with RVs. We really didn't know what we were doing most of the time (side note: give RV's lots of room on the road and never pull in front of one quickly; it's not easy to stop seven-plus tons of motion).

To say that Joe and I drive very differently is an understatement. Joe enjoys driving fast and tailgating. I prefer taking my time and giving myself plenty of room for other drivers to make mistakes. Our *stuff* inside the RV goes flying everywhere if we have to slam on the brakes. I hate that feeling, so I avoid it by driving passively and giving myself plenty of distance between other drivers and me. I meander up to a stop sign or light. Joe approaches a light as if it's going to change to green before he gets there.

Joe waits longer to apply the brakes than I do and likes to stop the RV right on another cars bumper. Why? Because he can. And the fact that our RV is a Class A with huge windows and no nose means we can get so close to another car that we can read their speedometer from our RV. Just kidding, but we are really close—again, my perspective.

On the first day on the road, Joe was driving. I noticed my anxiety begin to rise the longer he drove. My first thought was to ask him to drive like I do, because, after all, *my way is better,* right? Seems that way to me. What I wanted to do was *control* Joe's driving because I was afraid he was going to crash our "home."

Since I've been practicing all of the concepts I'm teaching in this book for many years, I was able to recognize that it was *not* my place to tell a 46-year-old man how to drive, even though *I* was fearful. I reminded myself that Joe hadn't had a car accident for most of his adult life and he only had a few speeding tickets in his lifetime. I decided that Joe didn't need to change; I did! So, I got up from the passenger's seat, moved away from the stimuli that was causing me to suffer to the couch where I couldn't *see* what was going on, and I took out my computer to do some work. Ahh peace!

Within a few minutes, Joe asked me why I had moved. I told him that I noticed I was becoming anxious about his driving style, which I assured him was not the *real* problem; I just prefer a different style of driving. (To be totally honest here, what *I* prefer is *my* driving because *I*, like you, want to be in control. Because *I*, like you, think that *I* do it better. And *I*, like you, feel safer when I'm behind the wheel—aka in control.) Now, doesn't that sound arrogant to you? It certainly does to me. Is that even the truth? Do I drive better than anyone else? Am I safer because I'm behind the wheel? Nope, not even close.

After I told Joe how I was feeling, his response was priceless; he said, "Oh Honey, I will back off and slow down. I'd rather have you up here with me." What? Double bonus!! Not only did Joe change his driving style to comfort me, but he also let me know that he desired me to be close to him. Joe made the choice to change *his* driving; I didn't have to ask him, or nag him, or try to convince him why *my* way was better than his way (which isn't—except in my own mind).

By now you might be wondering, "What if he didn't respond that way?" Then, I would have been perfectly happy working on my project until it was time for me to drive.

Joe and I have been traveling in our RV for over two years now. He has changed his driving style, mostly because he has done a lot of *Spiritual* growth and doesn't feel the need to drive aggressively anymore. He tends to be more aggressive in our Mini Cooper because it's fun for him to drive that way. Either way is fine with me now that I have figured out a way to adjust my perspective, both in my mind and in my location; we have never had an accident, and we have only had a few broken items in the RV from needing to stop quickly. *Big Smile*

There is *never* a good reason to try to control the behavior of an adult. There may be times you need to remove yourself or your children from danger, but you can do that without trying to control the other person or becoming frustrated with them.

Example:

Once my ex-husband's drinking became a serious issue, I decided it was in our best interest (we had a young child at the time) to ask Tim to leave our home if he chose to continue to abuse alcohol. While I couldn't stop Tim from drinking, I told him he was free to drink all he wanted just not around our son and me. Either he would willingly leave, or I would leave with our son. Because Tim wasn't ready to stop drinking, he chose to leave. I wasn't about to attempt to control Tim, but I could control what was in the best interest of my son and myself.

Example:

It seems to me that it takes women longer to get ready to leave the house than it does men. I'm not certain on the statistics, but I also think that *most* (not all) men are more conscientious about being places on time; the opposite may be true in your relationship. It doesn't really matter who's the "late one;" in most relationships there seems to be at least one person who can't manage their time accordingly (no judgments here by the way).

I have a friend whose wife is never ready when they need to leave if they are going to get to their destination on time. Now, what do you think typically occurs for this couple? Yup, Hubby gets upset and starts nagging the wife to hurry up, reminding her that she is always making him late, and asking why she can't seem to get out the door on time. Nine times out of ten, they end up having an argument while the wife is *still* getting ready or on the way to their destination.

What's another option for the husband? By the way, the husband here is not a victim to his wife's tardiness. How could the husband take responsibility for getting to the destination on time without nagging or complaining?

Here was my advice to this man: I told him that we *train* each other on what to expect from us and what we are willing to tolerate in our relationships. I suggested it might take a few times, with a new behavior from *him,* to better support his own value of being on time, but in the end they would both be happier. I told him to let his wife know what time they had to leave the house for the next event and that *he* would be leaving at that time. (Each of us has control over ourselves, and that's it!) He could tell his wife that if she isn't ready when they need to leave, she could meet him at the event without any irritation or resistance from the him—just a statement of his intentions. If it is important for his wife to drive to the event *with* her husband, she will be ready. If it's not that important, she can arrive any time she chooses, and she alone would bear the consequences of being late—whatever those might be. Regardless, there is no pressure; there is no fighting. There will likely be resistance at first as your partner is learning your new way of handling this issue. Ultimately, there is peace, and everyone gets to do what is most important to them. If there is only one car in the family, his wife can call a cab or she can miss the event. At some point, if it becomes important for his wife to either be on time to an event or to ride with her husband, she will make the necessary adjustments to her time management so she is ready when her husband wants to leave. That man can now be in a place of personal power *and freedom*—and so can his wife; no one is controlling the other. How easy-breezy is that, My Friend?

Example:

A client of mine, Sarah, told me that she believed that being her husband's wife of 10-plus years gives her the right to tell her husband, Robert, what she doesn't want him doing. Wrong! Very wrong! Unless she wants her husband to bolt someday. Where in the world did she get *that* idea?

I think it would be helpful to share this story with you because I imagine *most* women would have a problem with this situation, and if you can see my perspective *here* you will likely not have an issue with this principle of *freedom* that I'm teaching in this chapter.

You see, Sarah's husband is a professional photographer—a really amazing photographer! He has a very unique talent for photographing nudes in strikingly strange environments which, from my perspective, are very artistic but not pornographic, just strangely beautiful. They actually make me experience various emotions including empathy, sorrow, joy, and they are a bit mysterious.

Sarah feels threatened about Robert photographing nudes so she "won't let him." Robert does it anyway; he just keeps it from her so she doesn't get upset (also not a good idea). Much of the time the fruit of control is rebellion, lying, and withdrawing, rather than actually changing the unwanted behavior from our partners. In my opinion, the fruit of control is far worse than the unwanted behavior!

My lover Joe, is also an amazing photographer, and he has always wanted to photograph nudes since he was in high school. What high school boy doesn't want to photograph naked women, right? Only, Joe's desire never waned all these years; he had always wanted to be a fine-art nude photographer. The problem was, when he was married to his ex-wife, she also told him she didn't want him to photograph nude women because of *her* insecurities. Joe complied with her wishes, but he resented her for imposing on his *freedom* of choice—just another nail in the marriage-coffin. Before I continue with the story, let me say this about that. Joe resented the wrong person. If there were someone to resent or be mad at it would be himself. Joe should have recognized that *he* agreed to limit his photography experience, his ex-wife didn't "make" him do anything. If we do something out of obligation or to avoid conflict, it's called, "performing." Performing always leads to resentment. If we do something out of compassion, or for the best interest of another, that is being authentic. When we are authentic, we are peaceful and content with our decision and there is unity in the relationship.

So, what is this control about? It's about each of these ladies' fears. Which fears? Their *own* insecurity. I'm pretty sure I can speak into this since I'm a 56-year-old woman with a few *insecurities* of my own. By the way, who's issue is *my* insecurity? Mine, right?

I knew from the beginning of my relationship with Joe that he had always wanted to photograph nudes, so I encouraged him to do so, *in spite of my fears.* My fears are *not* Joe's issue, they are mine. I told Joe that if by him photographing nudes he ended up leaving me for one of his models, then he would have ended up leaving me for a younger more beautiful woman at some point anyway. Why not find out what's in this man's heart sooner rather than later? Joe is the only one who would know if he were putting our relationship at risk by photographing nudes, and, if so, he is responsible for governing his own choices for what is most important to him.

As it turns out, Joe is also an amazingly creative photographer of nude women. Joe suggested that I go with him on his nude shoots, which was thoughtful and supportive. I have gone with him on all of his nude shoots and discovered that he approaches these sessions with so much respect, dignity, and creativity. His portraits are stunning, and I love watching him work.

In my opinion, attempting to control our partners not only undermines the relationship with disrespect, but it also closes down the opportunity to see what's driving our own fears. Worst of all, it shuts off *our* opportunity to address and heal the fears that are limiting *our* lives. Once again, in my relationship with Joe, I chose to face my insecurities, take my fears to *Spirit*, and become a more empowered, confident woman, rather than remain crippled by my insecurities. Joe's desire to photograph nudes was *my* gift and became *my* opportunity to work on a dormant fear. It's so fascinating to me that Joe no longer photographs nudes. Perhaps that experience didn't hold the expectation he had of it, or maybe he just needed to know he had the *freedom* to do that if he wanted to. Either way, giving Joe the *freedom* to choose what was important to him supported "Us."

Example:

I had a client whose wife continually tried controlling her husband's behavior by complaining and criticizing him. Her controlling behavior caused such a distance between them that he was no long attracted to her sexually and began having affairs to satisfy the closeness he was missing with his wife. While my client didn't want to divide his family, he employed a strategy to get his sexual needs met so he could stay in his marriage. I'm certain his wife would be devastated to learn of her husband's infidelity. I'm also quite certain she would never have imagined that by trying to control some minor behaviors in her husband he would have chosen to cheat on her. Very few people realize the devastating impact of trying to control another person because the effects are quite subtle initially.

All of our choices and words either support and nurture our romantic relationship or weaken and dismantle it. We must be mindful of our impact and make the choices that are in the best interest of our lovers and guard the passion in our romantic relationship.

Dear Friend, address your fears *with* your lover. You will gain intimacy and security, as well as deepen your trust and *Love* for one another. In my relationship with Joe, *I decided to face my fear of losing him rather than lose him as a result of my fears.* We manifest our fears; they don't just appear out of nowhere! Control undermines a relationship—but only 100 percent of the time!!

Does this make sense, My Friend?

I want you to pay close attention from now on to the impact that control has, on men especially; this dynamic makes me sad. It emasculates men and makes them feel disrespected. Women seem to tolerate external control longer, but eventually, we too will resist it. We need to remind ourselves that our partner somehow survives when we aren't there to tell them what to do, where to park the car, how fast or slow to drive, how to get from point A to point B (unless they're asking), etc. At the end of the day, none of us want to have a romantic relationship with our controlling parents; we want lovers—amazing, supportive lovers!

We must give our lovers all the *freedom* to make their own choices just like we want to do. Remember, we learn from our successes *and* mistakes, not from other people controlling us. It works far better to become observers and students of the mistakes and successes of others. We need to encourage people, empower them, praise their successes, and listen openly to their point of view, as well as to their fears. We must accept them where they are, for who they are, in the process of evolution at *their* own rate, and respect them as wonderful, beautiful gifts from *God*.

Example:

The process of writing, printing, publishing, and creating an online presence to market a book takes a lot of time, talent, and effort. Much of this process I was not equipped for, so I needed help. Joe could do everything I couldn't, but he was also working on his projects; time was a major issue. While Joe had full intentions of taking care of the online details, I noticed that other things continually took precedence over my project's needs. Rather than resisting the schedule Joe was on, I decided to give these tasks a deadline in my mind. After two weeks of observing where Joe spent his time, without any progress on my project, I decided to hire out the work I needed finished. One morning I announced to Joe that I was going to hire out the final steps to getting *Our* book and website ready to launch. I never nagged him or complained about the lack of progress on my project; I simply took notice of his choices and my desires. I never had a twinge of fear regarding my, *I don't matter story,* because I've done the work of healing that emotional button. I also didn't have an ounce of resentment or frustration; Joe would have felt that!

Whose project is this book I'm writing anyway? Mine! Whose issue was getting this project finished? Mine! I could tell Joe was surprised at my statement about hiring someone, but he smiled at me and seemed relieved that I had taken control and made a decision to complete the project another way. About an hour later Joe thanked me "for being so awesome." When I asked what I had done, he told me that I didn't complain about him not working on my project, and I didn't even try to push him into getting the work done. He said he had spent the last hour kicking his own ass about not following through with his word, and it was a really great opportunity to look at other areas of his life where he wasn't following through. I never said a word! Had I tried to control the situation by complaining or nagging, he would have responded with resistance and he would have shut down, and I would have injured "Us." The *Love* and gratitude on this man's face was priceless. Joe thanked me for modeling behaviors for him that work so perfectly to support a *Loving,* safe, and passionate relationship. My Friend, this approach works beautifully to have the results we long for— to experience a *Real Passion Revolution* in these precious relationships.

Oh, and, by the way, Joe went on to edit half of my book. He *Lovingly worked on* my website videos, designed my Twitter page, designed my logo and my business cards without me saying one word. Joe is participating in ways I never asked for or dreamed he would. The gratitude in my heart is overwhelming at times! I really can't do enough for this beautiful man to thank him for his kindness and generosity.

Dear One, take a close look at your current reality regarding your intimate relationship; are you close or distant? If there is distance, then I'm certain you have been using control-behaviors in your relationship to get him/her to change. The side-effects of controlling behaviors are often even less favorable than the behavior we are trying to change.

We also need to step back and take a look at our own choices to see if we have been allowing our partner to control us. If so, we can address this with them and let them know with compassion that it's time for a change—a wonderful change!

Contrast the 7 *Deadly Behaviors* with Dr. Glasser's *7 Loving Behaviors* which support *Real Passion Revolution* in any relationship: (1) *Encouraging* (2) *Listening* (3) *Accepting* (4) *Trusting* (5) *Respecting* (6) *Empowering* (7) *Negotiating*

We need to learn to think outside the box when it comes to our romantic relationships. We must ask ourselves, "What do *I* long for in this relationship?" because, as I've already said, *that* is likely what is also needed and wanted by your partner. My answers to that question are: I want to be *Loved* and encouraged to be my best self, regardless of my occasional misses. I want my lover to empathize with my disappointments, frustrations, or sorrow. But, I want him to also give me an empowering perspective to shift my emotions and restore my peace and joy. I want my lover to ask me questions rather than make assumptions. I want my lover to see beyond my ego into my *Spirit* and empower my *True Identity* with words of affirmation. I want my lover to respect my freedom of choice—regardless of my choices. I want him to put his faith in God regarding my personal growth, and in me, so that I will discover what needs to be addressed in myself to experience an elevated life. I want my lover to be my best friend, my greatest fan, and my loudest cheerleader, so I offer all of that support to him. We are both so *grateful* for the *Loving* support we are receiving from each other that we *look* for ways to bless one another even more each day.

My Friend, if what you have been doing isn't working—regroup! The best way to do this is to sit down with your partner and tell him/her that you recognize you have been trying to control them because of *your* fears, then share *your* fears with him/her; that conversation alone will open up deeper connection and intimacy for both of you.

If you recognize you have harmed your relationship, ask for forgiveness and ask your lover how they felt when you did/said those things. Then ask for help with addressing your fears in a new way so your lover can participate in your healing.

We crave *freedom* in every aspect of our lives. Giving the gift of *freedom* in your romantic relationship is the path to experiencing a *Real Passion Revolution*.

I advise we all stick to the business that needs *our* attention the most: our own business!

One of the things you might be noticing after reading this section is how much fear is being flushed up at the thought of *not* having control of your partner. Relax, My Friend, you never did have control; you have only been destroying the passionate relationship you once had with your fearful, controlling behaviors. This concept is exciting, Dear One, because now you know the work that *you* need to do for your own happiness and for real peace—kick your fears out of your life!

The more we notice where fear is causing us to suffer and we make the shift from *fear to Love* through *Holy Healing*, the greater our sense of true *freedom*, peace, joy, and *Love* will be experienced *by us* and expressed *through us*. This, My Friend, is the *kingdom of God* that we are designed to experience. For sacred writings teach that the kingdom of *God* is within…is here…is available now.

I would like to address one last issue regarding trying to control your partner before moving on to the next section. I have made it very clear that it is not OK for anyone to attempt to control another adult, in particular, your lover. So, what if your partner wants to do something that crosses a personal boundary for you? For example, what if your lover decided that he/she wanted to be polyamorous (have multiple lovers), which is crossing a personal boundary for you? How could you handle that? Would it be OK to tell him/her that he/she couldn't do that? No! You could say that he/she was free to choose what he/she wanted, but so are you, and you wouldn't choose to stay in a romantic relationship with him/her if they wanted to be polyamorous. If experimenting sexually with other women/men was more important to your lover than your relationship, he/she would be free make that choice, but they would be giving you up as his/her lover. This would be an opportunity to discover what is most important for you both. Do you really want to manipulate your lover into being with you exclusively if they desire other sexual experiences? Where there's a will, there's a way! If it's in their heart to do that, they will figure it out. Wouldn't you rather be with someone who chooses you over everyone else every day because that's what they sincerely desire? I certainly would!

My Friend, you can have your deal breakers, your values, and your boundaries without imposing control strategies; just be clear with your lover what absolutely won't work for you. Many times we are willing to negotiate our differences, but there might be some things we simply won't, nor shouldn't, budge on. Those choices are very individual and personal for each of us.

Warning: be very careful not to use *boundaries* to try to manipulate your lover into behaving the way you want him/her to behave.

Example:

I know a woman who wanted her husband to make some changes in his behaviors. She told him that if he didn't change, she would file for a divorce. He wasn't sure he wanted to make those changes, so he moved out at her request. The wife filed for a divorce with the intention of getting his attention, assuming she knew him well enough after 30 years of marriage that he would want to keep his family together more than the changes she was insisting upon. She was painfully wrong! After moving out, this man discovered it was much more enjoyable not living with all of his wife's expectations, disappointments, and controlling behaviors (nagging and complaining). This man fell in love with another woman shortly after his wife kicked him out. To say she was shocked is an understatement! Two years later, she was still wondering what happened to dissolve her marriage so quickly. Manipulation and control dissolved her marriage. If that woman had this book in her hands and did the work I'm recommending, she would have discovered that her fear of financial scarcity was driving her to control her husband. She could have investigated the lies which drove her fears and made other, more *Loving* and supportive, choices. In doing so, this woman could have avoided that which she feared the most—a divorce!

What I have noticed in my relationship with Joe is that by eliminating control and implementing *Holy Healing* whenever my peace is disturbed, he desires me more and is compelled to make me happy in the ways he knows blesses me. When I don't resist his rate of personal evolution, he is able to recognize his own struggles without my help. When Joe is grumpy, which is rare, I don't need to say a word about his mood; I just remind myself he has his own demons to wrestle, as do I, and he will overcome them when he is ready. It's not my business; my business is to be true to myself, have integrity, do my own work, live my life with as few regrets as possible, and let *Love* flow regardless of the way others behave.

The result of this approach has blown my mind, which is why I am writing this book for you, My Friend! I am actually receiving everything and more that I have longed for in a relationship without ever needing to demand that Joe change one thing and without inflicting any harm on his *Spirit* or on *Us*. I want the whole world to have the same *Real Passion Revolution* that I am experiencing.

This process works! This is the Kingdom of *Love* we have been promised and have been created to enjoy. This is *Love* at its best! This is real life!

*SECRET INGREDIENT 7 CONCEPT: *Control vs Freedom*

1. Control is the fruit of unexamined fears.
2. Control destroys the passion in relationships.
3. Control is an illusion. We only have control of ourselves.

FAN THE FLAME

1. With whom do you recognize that you use controlling behaviors?

2. Who uses controlling behaviors to try to change you?

3. Which of the controlling behaviors do you use most?

4. Of the controlling behaviors that are used on you by others, which ones work? Which ones don't?

5. Which fears are you trying to address with control?

6. How have controlling behaviors harmed your relationship with your lover?

7. Now that you understand the damage you can cause by using *The 7 Deadly Behaviors* in your relationship with your lover, what is a better way to support your relationship AND address your fears in a way that is empowering and *Loving*?

Dear God of All— In All, Your ways are so much different than man's ways, and man's ways don't work. I desire freedom in every aspect of my life. Help me to recognize all the subtle ways that I attempt to control others and my environment to silence my fears. You alone are my resource for perfect peace. Draw me near, Sacred Spirit, that I may be whole, fulfilled, and happy.

And so it is, My Friend, and so it is!

Recipe Part 4

THE SPICES OF LIFE

Have you ever eaten a dish without enough salt or spices to make it come alive? You might as well eat cardboard; it's really boring and almost unpalatable. Just adding a few spices to a dish can transform it from dull to delish! Now, have you ever tried sea salt chocolate bars? Whoever figured out that adding course grain salt to chocolate, is brilliant in my opinion. It's only one ingredient but makes all the difference between boring and bursting with flavor! I believe *God* knew how boring it would be if we were all the same. Our uniqueness adds the right amount of spice to life if we are open and willing to accept that *our* way is not the *only* way to approach or experience life.

SECRET INGREDIENT 8

SPICY GENDERS

"Oh yes, you shaped me first inside, then out; you formed me in my mother's womb. I thank you, High God—you're breathtaking! Body and soul, I am marvelously made!"
Psalms 139:14 MSG

In the previous sections, I have stressed the importance of recognizing our *Oneness* to drop our judgments and work on our own issues, resulting in our healing and happiness. In this section, I will change my approach for dropping our judgments by sharing with you what I have learned about our *differences* that will support you in understanding the many ways we see and experience life uniquely. In this section, I will teach you about the less-obvious differences in our genders, our personalities, and our *Love* languages.

I find it fascinating when an event occurs, we can be in the same room, or come from the same family, or have the exact situation happen to us, and yet have an entirely *different* experience, or retell seemingly conflicting stories about the event/people. How is that even possible?

Because, Dear One, events are neutral, and each of us experiences life through our own set of filters designed around our unique personality type, our childhood *stories*, and our gender.

I found that when I learned these individual *differences,* I was able to change my mental filters to accommodate a variety of perspectives, which automatically opens up connection. I now relate to others easily by speaking a "language" *they* understand. I can connect with others on a deeper level because *they* feel understood and respected. This is a beautiful goal for all of our relationships—especially with our lovers.

Remember, My Friend, knowledge *applied* is power. If we want the best possible results in our most intimate relationships, then we must take the time to learn all we can to set ourselves up for success.

In *The Seven Habits of Highly Effective People*, Stephen Covey says, "Seek first to understand, then to be understood." If you haven't been exposed to this principle, let me tell you, it's quite powerful. As human beings, we long to be known and to feel like someone understands us, if only one person. The only way to really understand human behavior is to study it. What I am offering in this section are the summaries from my studies and experiences. Understanding these concepts will remove most of the relationship obstacles created by our unique individuality. This knowledge will create clearance for even more freedom and healing, leading you even deeper into a *Real Passion Revolution* with your lover.

While this is not an exhaustive discourse on human behavior, it has been sufficient to produce the favorable results I have had with my relationships and particularly with my companion, Joe.

MEN AND WOMEN

When I was in ministry with a dear friend of mine, Daniele Hage (www.dynamictraits.com), I supported her by attending all of the classes she taught regardless of how many times I had attended or how much I thought I understood the topic. As a result, I ended up taking her class on understanding men, *The Extraordinary Value of A Man (EVM)*, roughly twice a year for nine years. I'm so glad I did! I have got this stuff down now! Daniele also teaches a class about women for men called, *If Men Only Knew*. I have combined Daniele's teachings with my own findings from years of living in a household of all men. This information put into action has had a significant impact on my relationships with men. It has been profoundly evident when applied to Joe. I have heard Joe tell his friends many times how awesome it is that I totally understand him as a man and how easy it is to be in a relationship with me because of it.

I'm not sharing this with you to brag; after all, I simply *applied* what I learned. I'm sharing this with you because it works! And, I want you to experience the beautiful relationship that both you and your lover long for. You won't be able to have that relationship without understanding the gender-specific needs of both men and women.

Dear Friend, I want to be clear with you. I believe men and women are equals and should be considered equally in every relationship. I do not think that men should lead and women should follow. I believe we are One, first and foremost, as well as partners. I find it works best when we support each other in the most Loving ways. We each bring diverse strengths and unique perspectives into our relationship which are equally necessary to have the best possible balance in life. The concepts you are about to read are some of the ways we can best support the men and women in our lives (all of them) and, in turn, create an environment which empowers us to enjoy a Real Passion Revolution in our intimate relationships.

These are the insights I have learned from years of study and I use every day. Please consider these as general broad strokes regarding men and women. If you or your lover don't fit a particular profile, then you are the exception to these rules.

MEN AND RESPECT

This is perhaps the biggest obstacle in romantic relationships because women simply don't realize the plethora of ways men perceive disrespect. For example, did you know that telling your man how to drive or where there is an available parking spot is disrespectful and emasculating for a man? If you are ever in a car with two men, the passenger male will rarely, if ever, say a word about his compadres driving, speed, or parking. We ladies can learn a bunch from observing the way men interact with each other. They get the "bro-code" because they are the same species.

Men feel *respected* when we acknowledge their ideas, listen to them with the intent to sincerely understand *them*, and accept them right where they are without an agenda to change them. They feel *respected* when we consult them on decisions, affirm them, keep their secrets within the relationship, talk about their strengths and *Loving* acts publicly, and give them the freedom to make choices without any resistance, correction, or caution. Men feel *respected* when we allow them to grow at their own rate. It's critical that we not assume that we know what our men should or shouldn't be doing. Women do not think like men, process like men, or have the same needs as men in many areas of life.

Example:

I never interrupt a man when he's talking; it's very disrespectful! Ladies, I invite you to pay close attention to how frequently women interrupt men and then watch how the man responds to being interrupted; they shut down. Most men will not fight for the floor unless they are in a heated argument.

If Joe and I are with another couple and the male partner is interrupted by the female partner, I will *not* acknowledge what the woman said, and I will ask the man to continue his thought. That tells the man that I *respect* what he has to say, and it is a covert invitation to the woman to listen as her partner is speaking. I am not reinforcing a behavior in the woman that I know causes division in their relationship. I am modeling behavior for my female friend that will best support both her and her partner without reprimanding her (which would be totally inappropriate for me to do to another adult).

Most of us would agree that women tend to talk more than men. Most men are simply less verbal, so, when a man has decided to say something women would be wise, kind, and *respectful* to listen up, give them the floor, and allow them to finish their thought. What women tend to do is either interrupt a man mid-sentence or as soon as they take a breath. Give your man space to pause to think as he is formulating his perspective and then ask him questions or ask him to expound on what he just shared to be sure you have heard everything that is on his mind. Simply by asking, "What else honey?" or "Tell me more about _____" is enough to further his thoughts and for him to feel both heard and *respected*.

Let's be honest here ladies, most of us have so much to share we aren't actually listening to gain understanding; we are listening for a break in the conversation so we can talk again. If you are still doing that, I encourage you to refer back to Secret Ingredient 6 on effective communication skills.

Notice that men rarely interrupt another man; they listen quietly and wait patiently for their friend to say everything that is on his mind, even if there are several silent moments during his conversation. Men never really feel pressure to fill up all the empty space with words like women do.

Men feel disrespected and emasculated when women treat them like children. Consider this question: Is there any other adult that you would tell what to do or attempt to control besides your lover or perhaps your adult child? Why not? Because instinctively you know that it's really none of your business and entirely inappropriate to try to control another adult. My Friend, if you do this, you will eventually find yourself isolated from your man, and if you have sons, they will resist spending time with you too.

John Eldridge has written a series of books about men and their core needs. I strongly recommend that women read these books if they want to understand men deeply. In his book, *Wild at Heart,* John explains that he couldn't figure out why he had so much resistance being around his mother when he became an adult. One day he noticed that he felt like a little boy whenever he was around his mom. The reason he felt that way is because his mother framed him as her "little boy." Without realizing it, his mother was emasculating him, which made him feel small and powerless. Of course, for John, this was merely a *button* which needed his attention to bring the truth to the experience. But that doesn't alter the fact that his mother was (innocently) out of line, nor does it change the fact that he resisted being around his mother. No mother wants that result.

Example:

When my oldest son, Jonathan, was preparing to leave for military duty in Iraq during the height of the war, his grandmother asked him to promise to be safe. Jonathan's response was abrupt and bluntly clear. He said, "Grandma, I can't promise that I will be safe. I have to be brave and protect the men I am responsible for, which means I probably won't be safe." What he needed from her, and everyone, was the affirmation that he was fully equipped to do his job well. He wanted to hear that we all believed in him to save lives when it was in his power to do so and that we were profoundly proud of him for this act of service to our country.

You see, ladies, the deepest fear men wrestle with is the question, "Am I enough? Do I really have what it takes to make it as a man in this world?" Our lover needs us to be their cheerleader who is continually pointing out his strengths. Trust me, men are acutely aware of their weaknesses, and they beat themselves up over them repeatedly. No one is harder on a man than himself. If you want your man to thrive and be his best self, authentically affirm him—a bunch, every chance you can, every time it's appropriate! If you want the relationship to end, treat him like a child and disrespect him publicly.

I had a client ask me if she should fake respect for her husband because honestly she didn't respect him. So I began to explore with her the possible things she *could* respect her husband for. I said, "Heather, does your husband go to work every day?" She replied, "Yes." I asked, "Is the money he brings home significant for the lifestyle you currently enjoy?" "Yes," she said. Then I said, "I wonder why you dismiss these things as something you would respect him for?" She said, "Oh, he's supposed to do that." You see, Heather's focus was on what he *wasn't* doing to meet her needs rather than on what he *was* doing.

If you have a challenging relationship and struggle to find good things to respect about your lover, I suggest you ask people who know him well what they see and respect in him. Many times we are blinded by disappointments (unmet expectations) and can't see clearly. Whenever we find ourselves in a judgment of our lover (or anyone else) the little attorney in our brain will go about gathering evidence to make us right about those judgments. We will completely miss or dismiss whatever evidence is there that doesn't support our case.

If you want your relationship to be safe and passionate, build your man up by showing him *respect* in whatever ways are significant for him. If you aren't sure how to do this, ask him, "Honey, in what ways can I show you *respect*?" If you want to know how he perceives disrespect ask him, "Honey, do you ever feel disrespected by me? If so, how do I do that?" Most men are more non-verbal about being disrespected, so much so that their entire body will shout, "Stop!" Men either shut down completely or get enraged when they're being disrespected. If you are paying attention to your man's verbal and non-verbal communications, you won't even have to ask when he feels disrespected.

WOMEN AND SECURITY

Many of you women reading this book might not recognize this as a woman's greatest need, but programmed into our primal brain is the knowledge that men are physically stronger than women, and the world is full of dangerous elements that men are better equipped at overcoming than women. Centuries ago, women were dependent upon men to capture and kill the food for their family, cultivate the soil for produce, protect them from the dangers of wild animals or enemies, and build a shelter for them and their children.

We women are far more independent today, but our need to feel a sense of *security* remains the same. I find it interesting that while many women are self-sufficient these days with equal job opportunities, education, and income, most women still feel more peaceful and *secure* having a man in their life who will *Love* them and protect them from danger.

The greater challenge for many women is feeling *secure* in their relationship. By "secure" I mean that the relationship is not at risk from an outside intruder. You see, gentlemen, we understand that men are visually attracted to women. We have believed the media messages that what all men want is a beautiful, fit, young woman to have as much sex with as he desires. Whether that is *entirely* true or not, that media message puts women at high risk in our minds! Why? Because we have yet to discover the fountain of youth. We are getting older, our bodies change, and there will always be more beautiful, youthful women around. There is no getting around that fact!

I have heard many men complain about the extremes women will put themselves through to keep the appearance of their youth through plastic surgery without considering *why* women would even put themselves at risk for those procedures. Just as men have an innate impulse to be visual creatures, women have an innate desire to please men visually.

Ladies, don't throw this book out of the window yet; allow me to explain.

In 2014 there were 15.6 million elective plastic surgical procedures performed in the United States, an increase of 3% from 2013, despite the economic struggles we currently face. Women are merely responding to what we *think* men are looking for. I believe the evolution of plastic surgery is mostly about women trying to conform into the image they *perceive* men want. When a man makes a comment about another woman's big boobs or firm booty, women think, "Oh, bigger/firmer is better; this is what men want." While women can work out for a firmer butt, we can't work out for bigger boobs, so off to the plastic surgeon we go. Women are constantly *listening* for what men desire so they can do their best to conform themselves into that perfect image that will finally get them the *security* they long for. Just look at the evolution of the female lips. Ever consider why a woman would inject filler to distort her lips so much? They are simply responding to what they believe men *desire*. Keep this word "desire" in mind as I will tell you shortly how significant it is for most women.

Of course, not all women feel this way, nor would many women put themselves at risk physically to reduce their chances of abandonment. But, many women do. I believe many more women would have plastic surgery given the financial resources to do so. According to a survey conducted by CouponCabin.com, 23 percent of more than 2,500 U.S. adults polled said they would consider plastic surgery if costs were lower.

Women have the propensity to compete with other women for the attention/affection of men. Women dress *for* men *and* to compete with the other women who might be in their space. We have a need to "win" in a way that men don't! So, how can men best support their women to feel *secure*? While most of a women's sense of security is a personal work of interrupting the internal dialog which tells them they aren't beautiful enough, men would be wise to reduce their woman's anxiety about their *security* by affirming them frequently. Genuine affirmations will usually calm a woman's fears and help her override her tendency to be self-critical. But, gentlemen, if your woman has significant poor self-esteem, and especially body image issues, it won't matter how much you tell her she is beautiful there won't be any place for those words to land in her *Spirit.* More than likely, she spent the day filing away all the evidence she could find to the contrary—that she isn't pretty enough! A woman's self-esteem is her issue, and no man can *fix* that for her.

MEN ARE VISUAL

Let's go there! This is a struggle for many women, but if we can gain an understanding of this male trait, we can not only have a sense of peace about it, but a sense of humor about it too. In this way, we can be supportive rather than destructive with our men in spite of their innate propensity to look at beautiful women.

Men are visual beings for several primal survival reasons. (1) Men developed heightened visual awareness to be able to see prey to adequately protect and feed their families. (2) Men are prewired to procreate with a healthy woman for healthy offspring. A curvy young woman is a sign of fertility; a woman with shiny hair means healthy offspring.

Asking a man not to look at other women is like asking a woman not to comfort a crying baby; we *have* to, ladies, it's part of our DNA! Just because a man looks at another woman and even seems to be enjoying the view, doesn't mean he wants to trade you in for her. It simply means he is a man! Dogs bark at intruders. Lions eat other animals. Fish swim. Bears _____ in the woods. Men look at women.

In *Working With The Law,* Raymond Holliwell teaches the "Law Of Non-Resistance." This principle states that our suffering comes from resisting "what is" (the current reality) rather than being at peace with it. Throughout history, women have been trying to get the men in their lives to stop looking at other women through nagging, complaining, shaming, and punishing. Ladies, please don't shame your man for being a man. Would you shame a fish for swimming or a dog for barking at an intruder? Even if your man agreed with you and tried to stop looking at other women, he would be lying if he said he never looked at women when you weren't around.

The best way to secure your relationship is *not* to try to stop your man from looking at other women, but to be a *Loving*, supportive, encouraging, nurturing, playful, sensual, confident lover. *That* will keep him captivated with you regardless of how beautiful another woman might be. How do you get there? Take your fears and insecurities to *Spirit* for a new perspective through *Holy Healing*, Sweetheart.

"If you can't beat 'em, join 'em!" I recommend you join your man (non-resistance) and not only make it OK to admire other women, but make it more fun for both of you. Many women are beautiful to look at and admire for their beauty. I believe we are *all* drawn to beauty in whichever form that takes—including beautiful men *and* women. I'm usually the one to point out a beautiful woman to Joe. First, because he has been conditioned that *looking* is bad, so he would never point out a beautiful woman to me. And second, because I truly appreciate women with beautiful hair, eyes, fashion, bodies, and confidence.

Example:

My client, Brian, recounted an experience to me that he had with his girlfriend, Allison, who had scolded him several times for looking at other women. Later that evening Allison made a comment about wanting to have sex, which Brian said was the furthest thing from his mind. He said Allison's insecurity completely turned him off—precisely the opposite of what she wanted. Brian stated that if Allison had joined him in admiring the woman he saw it would have turned him on so much he would have wanted to have sex with her right there. Most women love to be the object of our man's desire; it's a win-win ladies!

My Friend, *we* create that which we fear! Allison's fear wasn't that her lover would look at other women. Her deepest fear was that if Brian found the other woman more beautiful, he would want to be with her rather than with Allison. At the end of that particular day, Brian didn't want to be intimate with Allison. Not because of the other woman, but because of *Allison's reaction* to her own fears. Does this make sense?

This point bears repeating: Trying to control your man from looking at other women is a sign of insecurity, which is unattractive to men. This is the opposite of what you want in your relationship with your lover! If you want to gain your man's admiration and attraction, affirm him in his visual instincts. He isn't going to leave you for it, but he just might leave you for nagging or shaming him about an instinct he was given in his natural development of becoming a man.

MEN AND AFFIRMATION

My Friend, if you want your man to be the best version of himself, you need to cultivate the powerful language of *affirmation*—even if it feels awkward at first. This is a beautiful gift to give everyone. We can all develop the language of *affirmation*. I believe the majority of people appreciate being, and need to be, *affirmed*. However, the impact is different for men and women. In men, it causes him to feel empowered to slay the dragons in his world, conquer his fears, and pursue his biggest dreams. In women, it gives her the feeling of security in her relationship, which frees her mind to be creative, confident, and peaceful.

Example:

Joe and I attended an event where there was a DJ and dancing. I *Love* to dance! I *Love* to dance! Did I mention that I *Love* to dance?! So I danced a while with Joe, with his daughter, and with a few strangers. At the end of the evening, the DJ approached me and shared with me how my dancing had a significant impact on him and on many others as he observed the energy in the room change from one of low energy to one of high energy once I got up to dance. The DJ actually thanked me for dancing! He then continued to *affirm* me for another 15 minutes in various ways. What I noticed was the impact his words had on me. I was drawn to this his friendly, kind, positive, *Loving* energy. I felt seen, valued, and appreciated by a stranger. The gift of his *affirmations* blessed me for several days after that event. I told Joe that I wanted to be more aware of the many times and ways that I could give the gift of *affirmations* to people I meet. I want others to have the same beautiful experience with me that I had with that DJ. I want to be known as someone who notices *and* voices the beauty in others and as an encourager of the gifts they unknowingly share with the world!

Affirming your lover, or anyone, can feel strange at first. I found, in the beginning, there was a sense of vulnerability for me in *affirming* others. But, I want to encourage you to push through those uncomfortable feelings and do it anyway. Through practice, this will become very natural for you and you will *feel* the blessing you are to those around you who desperately need to hear that they are valuable in this world.

As I mentioned earlier, a man's biggest secret is that he feels inadequate for the task of being a man. Often he is living up to the image of his father, or other men whom he perceives *are* equipped. Additionally, he sees Hollywood's images of men like William Wallace in *Braveheart*, Maximus in *Gladiator*, or Hawkeye in *The Last of the Mohicans*. This is the equivalent of women living up to the photoshopped models in fashion magazines.

Men perceive *affirmation* as respect and feel empowered by it to slay the necessary dragons to further their careers, make their dreams a reality, and build a kingdom for their queen and their family to dwell in safety. Men want to hear that you see them doing their best. Your man cannot hear from you often enough that you believe in him. Men want to be told they are beautiful, strong, intelligent, and creative. Joe *Loves* it when say how beautiful he is and how much I *Love* the man that he is. He gets the biggest smile on his face whenever I tell him how *Loved* I feel and how happy he makes me because that means he is doing "it" right. I pay attention to as many details as I can as I observe his choices throughout the day. I thank him for the things he does that I know aren't his favorite things to do but are necessary. I thank him for the things he does that make my life with him so amazing. I also praise him for the brother he is, the son he is, the father he is, the businessman he is, and the friend he is.

One of the primary reasons men cheat on their wives is because they aren't getting a "win" at home. If the sweet young lady at the office is praising your lover and showering him with respect and *affirmations*, he is "winning" at work. If he then goes home to a complaining, nagging, unhappy wife (remember, our happiness comes from within not from others), he is losing at home. He will likely linger at the office to get the *affirmation* and respect he needs.

If we spend our time looking and listening for ways to *affirm* our lovers, there won't be any space to be critical of them. Did you know that it is impossible to be grateful and critical at the same time? One tool Joe and I use to exercise our "gratitude muscle" is with prayer beads. We currently use Mala beads that a dear friend made for us. They work well for our gratitude practice. You could use Rosary beads or even a pearl necklace. The process is simple: each bead represents something to give thanks for. I strongly recommend doing this gratitude practice first thing in the morning to begin your day with a heart filled with gratitude. Many times I take my beads for a walk on the beach where I give thanks for creation in its many beautiful, mysterious forms—including my darling lover, Joe.

I believe that underneath our struggles and messiness is beauty and brilliance. I believe we are all doing the best we can everyday with what we understand. I often speak of the covert gifts in Joe. I do not exaggerate or inflate his characteristics, but there are things I notice in Joe that he doesn't see in himself; I praise him for those things.

I believe that a universal lie so many of us need to interrupt is the lie that "we aren't enough." One way I am supporting Joe to interrupt that lie in his life is by telling him all the ways he is enough and even more than enough!

Darling, if you are going to experience a *Real Passion Revolution* in your life and have the fulfilling intimate relationship you dream of, you must become your lover's biggest cheerleader and greatest fan.

If you struggle to affirm your lover, I suggest that you consider there is likely an offense you are holding onto. We often will withhold affirmations as a form of punishment or to keep a distance in our relationships because we believe we have been wronged. For many people, giving the gift of affirmations makes them feel vulnerable. Typically, we only let down our guard and open ourselves up when we feel safe. So, if there are any unresolved issues in the relationship, it will be quite challenging to affirm your lover. I suggest you revisit Secret Ingredient 5 and do the work of forgiveness. Your relationship will not move forward without removing all of the obstacles of those lingering offenses. Fan the flame!

WOMEN AND DESIRE

This *need* goes hand in hand with women needing to feel secure. Gentlemen, the best way for your woman to feel secure in your relationship is to verbally and non-verbally let her know you are crazy about her and that she turns you on! A common mistake a man will make is to assume his woman knows that he's attracted to her because he is with her or because he wants to have sex with her. Guys, your woman assumes you would have sex with anyone that would let you. That doesn't make her feel special.

Men, tell your woman she is gorgeous, intelligent, resourceful, and a fantastic lover. Far too often you might say we are good cooks, kind, and thoughtful. We need to hear those first four affirmations from our lovers to feel desired and secure in our relationship. Also, never tell us we look "nice." No, no, no! Your mother, sister, co-worker, or neighbor looks "nice." Your lover is "sexy," "hot," and "drop dead gorgeous!" Do you hear the difference men? "Nice" is thoughtful to say, but the speaks of passion and *desire*! At this point, I'm sure I have the approval of most women reading this book.

There is an old joke about a man who was married for over 50 years. His wife asked him if he still *Loved* her because he never told her he did. His response was, "I told you I *Loved* you when I married you; if anything changes, I'll let you know." Sorry fellas, telling your woman once that she turns you on ain't even close to enough. She needs reassurance every time she gets dressed or undressed in front of you just like you need the reassurance that her respect and affirmations give you.

Example:

I remember a time when I was putting clothes together for a cruise with my ex-husband. I had recently lost twenty pounds, so I went shopping for something that would "wow" him. I tried it on to show it to Tim before packing. When I walked into our den, our nine-year-old son saw me and blurted out, "Wow, Mommy, you look so beautiful!" My husband was in another room, so I went to find him. He looked up from his newspaper and said, "Where did you get that dress?" Not quite the response I was hoping for! My heart sank. I went back to the den, picked up my son, and said, "Thank you, Ryan. Mommy needed that."

Here's a slightly different example. I'm going to refer to it as, "Plan B." Joe and I were at an event that I was dressed up for, and I was excited for Joe to see me in my new outfit; sound familiar? I was sure he would get quite excited, and I imagined words of affirmation would pour out of his mouth. I was wrong about a spontaneous verbal response from him, so I had a few moments of disappointment until…I released that expectation and tuned into all the other people who were affirming me.

While my greatest *desire* is to hear that Joe thinks I'm the most beautiful and desirable woman in the room, as I received the words of affirmation from others, I found myself quite fulfilled with their compliments. Joe affirms me in other ways that I have come to learn are his own language of attraction and *desire*.

I am constantly catching Joe *desiring* me from across the room with his eye contact, taking the time to pause to kiss me or hold me in his arms. He will dance with me while waiting in line for an event, or randomly caress me just because he *Loves* to touch me. All of these actions tell me that he *desires* me, and as a result I feel secure in our relationship. Joe tends not to be as verbal as he is physical, but I get the message through his physical attention; this is a *Love* language preference that I will expound on later in this section.

Can you see my point? Women need to *feel desired* by their lover to *feel* the sense of security she needs to experience a deep sense of peace. Besides, gentlemen, you and I both know that you are very attracted to women who are confident and happy. If you want to have a confident, happy lover, help her feel secure in her relationship with you. Communicate your admiration for her in as many ways as you can—her external and internal beauty. Women blossom in an atmosphere of affection and adoration; they wilt in silence and criticism. I believe this is the number one reason why women have affairs or leave a relationship. Leave your woman's need to *feel desired* unfulfilled, and another man will draw her away by doing what she longed for from *you*. Either you were unwilling to meet her need or ignorant of her needs altogether. Unfortunately, just like our judicial system, "Ignorance of the law is no excuse." We are each responsible to know the laws. We would do much better in our relationships if we took responsibility to understand these *Universal* laws of human behavior as well.

MEN ARE SINGLE-FOCUSED

Ladies, if your man is busy on a project, watching a sports game, researching on his computer, or playing with the children, do NOT interrupt him unless it's an emergency. Women are diversely focused and can usually shift quickly to address a question or any interruption without feeling irritated or disrespected in any way; not so for most men.

I have found that the most common reason a woman interrupts a man is because a thought popped into her head and she doesn't want to forget it. Ladies, develop the habit of writing all that stuff down if you're concerned you will forget, and talk to your man about it later. By the way, this is the most challenging concept for me to remember. I usually *remember* after I have said something to Joe without a response.

There have been times when I have started to talk to Joe only to abruptly stop myself because he didn't respond to my question or comment immediately. When I actually *looked* at him, I saw he was focused on something. When he then had a delayed response (because he heard a noise—my voice) I would say, "never mind honey, you're busy, we can chat later." This is one reason so many men prefer to be alone when they want to do something that requires their attention! If you enjoy just being in the same room with your lover like I do, I suggest you be a "silent partner" when your lover is focused on something.

A man is so single-focused it is impossible for him to both ignore you *and* do whatever he's doing; he is only focused on a task and didn't hear you. His brain is so absorbed in what he's doing that his ears have shut down. Even if he did hear a sound, his mouth can't form words to respond because his entire brain is engaged for survival on this one thing he is focused on. I know this sounds dramatic and a bit ridiculous, so I invite you to pay close attention to your man's body language the next time you try to interrupt him when he is focused on something. Sometimes Joe will not even hear a sound and is entirely oblivious that I just said something. Other times I watch him try to turn his head away from what he's doing but he can't, and then there is a long delayed response, "Huh? Did you say something?" Every time that happens I laugh at myself for even trying to say something, and I laugh at him for trying to disengage his activity to find out what I need.

So, what's a girl to do if she really does need her man's attention and he's focused on a project? Walk over to him and touch him on his shoulder and say, "Honey, (*long pause*) when you get a moment I need to talk to you about _____ (the kids, the house, the gardener, an appointment) fill in the blank. Be specific; do not say I need to talk to you about "something" because he will immediately think he's in trouble. If it's really urgent, tell him it's urgent. Men need a moment to shift their focus, or they will act like they are listening but won't be able to register what you're saying. And when you're done talking he will likely say, "What?" or, "Can you repeat that?" and then both of you will feel frustrated.

WOMEN MULTI-TASK

Women are the opposite of men in their world of focus; we have sharp peripheral eyesight and hearing. Women have the capacity to have many things going at the same time and not miss a beat with any of them. We can be fully aware of a load of laundry washing, the food cooking on the stove, when our kids need to be picked up, our dental appointments, the conversations we're having on the phone, and the kids playing in the backyard. Women can have several conversations going at the same time with other women in the room and keep track of them all. Most of the time, women can shift quickly without losing momentum or feeling frustrated.

The downside to being multi-focused is twofold: (1) We expect the other people in our lives to be multi-focused as well, so we don't understand why they [men] can't shift focus as easily as we can. As we just learned, men are single-focused; this innate difference between men and women can lead to frustration in a relationship if we aren't properly informed. (2) We can be so aware of so many things that need our attention that it's difficult for us to leave something undone, which can lead to burnout, depression, and, worst of all, no sex drive!

Men, did you know that the "things" in a woman's environment have voices that demand our attention? The kitchen sink is *begging* to be emptied of dirty dishes, the kids school project is sitting on the dining room table *requiring* attention, the bathtub is dripping water, and your woman hears it *crying* out for repair…and the beat goes on, and on, and on in her head. Most women can't pass by any undone chore in her home or place of work without stopping to address that perceived need, which is why she is often distracted from her original objective and onto another.

*Let me discuss a few ways men can support their multitasking lovers:

1. Remind them that you are a single-focused man and simply don't multitask well.

2. Realize that often the frustration you are observing in your woman is a hidden request for help, so ask her if there is anything you can do to ease her burden. Don't assume you know what she needs; ask her specifically.

3. Step in and take a few things off her plate if you notice she is burning the candle at both ends.

4. Remove her from her environment (work or home) to silence the voices that tell her she isn't done. I'm sure you've heard the saying, "A woman's work is never done" and now you know why. If you see your woman is tired but pushing through her list of demands, stand her up (if she's sitting), give her a hug, place your hand on her lower back or her arm, and lead her to the couch, or a hot bathtub, or outside, and invite her to sit for a few moments and relax; assure her she will have more energy to finish those tasks if she takes a break; tell her you will help her with _____ (be specific).

MEN'S NEEDS ARE URGENT

Men don't ask for help unless it's *critical or urgent.* When he is hungry, or tired, or horny, it's *urgent;* it really is a critical situation for them, which is why they get frustrated when their needs aren't met right away. The interesting thing about this trait is that they also believe that everyone else's needs are critical and urgent so they feel a pressure and urgency to fulfill any requests right away.

Women, on the other hand, are conditioned to put their needs aside to meet the needs of everyone else first.

Keep in mind that, "We don't see things as they are, we see things as *we* are." When you make a request your man will assume it's *critical and urgent* unless you state otherwise. His assumption will be that what you are asking him to do must be done right now, and he is likely deeply involved (single focused) with something else, even if it's a favorite TV show, and your request will irritate him.

If I need Joe's attention I will say something like, "Honey, when you get a chance I need your help with _____, but it's not urgent." If I needed his help right away, I'd say so; I can recall only one time in the last two years that my need was urgent.

You would be surprised at what a big deal it is for a man to have the space to be focused on a task without being interrupted. I believe one of the reasons Joe and I can live so blissfully in our 250-square-foot RV, spending most of our 24-hour days together, is because I understand all of these innate traits about men. Joe has the freedom to do what he needs to do and what he wants to do without being interrupted. The result is that he is more than eager to help me when I really need him.

WOMEN GATHER

Women gather thoughts and feelings much like they pick up toys and clothes around the house all day long. At some point, she *needs* to empty that basket, and her man needs to be the safest and strongest place for her to do that. A close girlfriend can be very supportive in a woman's life to help her empty her basket, and I strongly recommend a woman empty as much of her *stuff* with her friends. But there are things a woman wants to share only with her lover. This can be very challenging for men since they are programmed to get to the bottom line asap so they can *fix* whatever they perceive is wrong. For most women, there isn't anything that needs *fixing*, so I'm here to tell you men that you are off the hook; you don't need to *fix* a thing (except that leaking faucet). A man might think, "Then why are you telling me this if there isn't anything I can do for you?" Again, this is the innate difference between men and women. Women *need* to talk, to process out loud, to hear themselves talk, to feel heard and known for no other purpose than to empty those thoughts and feelings out of their bodies and minds. For most men, the purpose of talking or sharing is to get to a solution. It certainly isn't just for the purpose of talking! For many women, myself included, just hearing myself talk is enough to discover new insights and resolve many issues.

Women want to feel validated in their feelings and thoughts, so if a man will just listen quietly and affirm her by acknowledging her struggles or successes, then he has been a *Loving,* supportive partner to her, and she will *feel Loved* by him; this connection often leads to a woman wanting to have sex. So, gentlemen, if for no other reason, I recommend you spend time allowing your woman to empty her emotional basket. Consider it a form of foreplay!

Men, listen up! I mean listen with both ears to this critical part: Women are acutely aware when you are placating her—pretending to listen but not really present *with* her in the conversation. We know when you are listening because that is what you "should" be doing, and we are aware of when you are genuinely interested in our life behind the curtain. Remember, you suck at multitasking, so if your thoughts are somewhere else, your non-verbal communication is quite obvious to a woman. It would be best if you were honest and said you don't have the time or the mental energy to hear what she has to say right now than to pretend you are listening when you aren't. Whenever that has happened to me, I have shut down; I'm not going to waste my time and energy, or yours, talking to someone who doesn't care about what I'm sharing at that time. For me, that isn't a bad thing or frustrating; it simply is what it is, and I accept it as such. This form of honesty will likely push her "I don't matter" button, but that's OK, it's still the better option than performing—faking attention or interest. Your woman can walk away and go process that experience for some inner healing work and emerge a more empowered woman.

Let me encourage you once again to dive into the teachings of Byron Katie if you haven't already done so. She is a brilliant teacher, and I use her concepts all day long. Byron's work has spared me a lifetime of self-imposed suffering from faulty perceptions, and I am deeply grateful for her willingness to share with the world what has set her free!

MEN RESCUE

Men are born heroes and feel empowered, valuable, and respected when we ask them for their help. Men really do enjoy being needed *and* wanted. Some women are so fiercely independent that they do everything themselves, which leaves their man without an expression for the hero that lies within. Watch them light up when they are able to help a woman whom they perceive is in distress. Even young boys get excited when we tell them how helpful they are and find ways to let their inner hero get to work.

Example:

I recall a day when I was speaking at a seminar and had a car full of stuff to take into the facility. I could have done all the work myself, but I saw three men chatting nearby so I said, "Gentlemen, I'm running a bit late, I could sure use some strong men to help me if it's not too much trouble." Within seconds, I had all three men jump up and jog over to assist me. The smiles on their faces were priceless, and I praised them the entire time they were unloading my car. I recognized the look on their faces like the way I feel when I get the opportunity to make a difference in someone's life—that feeling of satisfaction for being of value to another person. I take as many opportunities as I see to ask for help from men as well as allow them to assist me whenever they ask if they can help me with something—like carry something for me, or put away my grocery cart. Ladies, if a man offers to help you, your answer is *always*, "Yes!"

My Friend, let me make a significant distinction here: there is a huge difference between needing your lover to help you and being *needy*. Asking a man to help with something when he is available or is offering to assist you is not perceived by men as a woman being "needy." I think that many women have misinterpreted the concept of coming across as being needy so they avoid asking men for help when they truly need help or accept help from a man just because he wants to help out. Don't neglect your lover's innate desire to feel needed and wanted, but don't abuse his disposition either. When a woman communicates that her lover is her *only* source of happiness or contentment, it puts too much pressure on her man, which makes him feel stressed; this is a needy woman. When a man feels smothered or controlled by a woman, it makes him want to bolt. Don't do that to him! When a woman is insecure or jealous, and she tries to control her lover's behavior to accommodate *her* insecurities, she is being needy. Neediness, ladies, is very unattractive to men.

MEN AND HAPPINESS

A man's goal in his relationship is to make his partner happy. Men feel responsible for their lover's happiness. Therefore, in his mind, if she is happy, he is successful. Now, I know this is a bit of a paradox given that I have already taught you that we are either happy or not because of the internal healing work we have done on ourselves and that the real sense of happiness comes from within not from without. Regardless, if a man sees an unhappy woman, he feels compelled to make her happy—think, "damsel in distress." Men are intensely attracted to happy women because when she is happy he can focus on other problems to solve. If a man perceives he isn't making his partner happy after many attempts, he will abandon the relationship.

Example:

Joe sincerely felt like he just didn't have what his ex-wife needed to make her happy. He genuinely wanted his wife to be happy, so he, in *Love*, released her from their marriage to find her happiness with someone who would be a better fit for her. This made perfect sense to Joe. His ex-wife was very confused by his response to end their marriage rather than try to fix it. From his perspective, he had already done everything he knew to make his wife happy for 20 years but had failed. So giving her a divorce was the most *Loving* act he could think of for both of them.

Ladies, if you want to keep your man, and you want a better life, do the work of healing your emotional wounds. Give yourself *and* everyone around you the gift of your own happiness. Remember, your happiness is not your lover's responsibility; it's yours!

I mentioned earlier that men require a "win" in their relationships and in business. If a man's partner is constantly correcting him or complaining that she is unhappy, the man will need to go elsewhere to get that "win." This is a survival strategy, not a weakness. By the way, most men are pretty relentless in their pursuit of their lover's happiness. If your man does leave, just know it was because he saw that there was no way he could make you happy. Remember, your happiness is *your* business, not his.

WOMEN AND CONNECTION

As I already shared in Secret Ingredient 6 regarding communication, a relationship is only as good as the ability to effectively communicate. Communication and relationship are synonymous! Communication is the ability to listen *without an agenda*, to speak clearly, to give and receive feedback, to negotiate preferences, and to share openly. The *quality* of a relationship can only be as good as the *quality* of the communication within that relationship. Women feel *Loved* when they feel known; this is the result of *quality* listening and sharing. Women feel connected when there is open communication. This can be challenging for men, who aren't nearly as verbal. Men have the propensity to stay in their heads, to think things through, and to edit their conversations so they don't say something that will upset their partner.

It's critical that we keep the experience of communication safe. By this, I mean that there isn't a *reaction* from either partner that would shut down the conversation. If the content is painful or challenging, it's essential that we stay open to hearing what our lover is sharing without defending ourselves, arguing with them, minimizing their experience, or dismissing their feelings. Equally important is not falling into self-judgment, telling ourselves we are bad, or shaming ourselves for doing something wrong which will ultimately have the same effect—shutting down communication. One way to easily and effectively keep conversations open and safe with your lover is a concept from the book *The Four Agreements, "Don't take anything personally."*

Remember the story I shared in Secret Ingredient 6 about Tim's body-language-reaction when I shared my longing to be affirmed by him? Once Tim shut down, I recall thinking, "Tim isn't safe for me to share what I need from him, so I will just keep my needs to myself." Because of Tim's wounds and judgments of himself, he didn't have the capacity to engage in quality conversations without being offended, so I stopped having those conversations with him. We all know by now that this relationship ended.

As I shared with you in the section on control vs freedom, withdrawing and blame are forms of control. If it's true that we train our partners how to be in relationship with us by our actions and reactions, then Tim got what he really wanted: a wife who stopped talking about things that he couldn't handle, which ultimately led to a divorce. If you don't want those results in your relationship too, then become a safe, quality communicator, both in listening and in sharing.

Example:

I told Joe that one of his behaviors that supports my sense of security with him is his level of honesty with me. I don't want Joe to edit his conversation with me, so that I don't get upset when he shares something with me that pushes a *button*. I told him that if he says something that pushes a *button* for me, it's not a bad thing! It's just an opportunity for me to take a look at a fear that lies in the shadows of my subconscious.

And that, My Friend, is always a beautiful opportunity for healing. I'm far less interested in staying comfortable than in becoming whole, continuing my *Spiritual* evolution, deepening my understanding of *Love* and humanity, and having a safe, passionate, empowering relationship. I know that healing, happiness, and a fulfilling life are the result of being willing to stand in the pain of what needs my attention.

Another way for women to feel *connected* is through participation *with* her lover. When men talk about their goals and dreams, women are inspired to support them and join in the adventure. I think the term "teamwork" best describes how a woman wants to engage with her lover. We want to do *Love* and life *together.*

Example:

As Joe and I have traveled America the past few years, I've become aware that I get the most enjoyment sharing each new experience *with* him. To see a beautiful sunset and share that moment *together* is a more heightened experience than if I were watching it by myself. To discuss an audiobook we are listening to or reading together is far more meaningful and powerful in my life than learning that material alone. I actually learn about a subject *and* about Joe through this kind of sharing.

Much of my adult life with my ex-husband (remember, I was married 33 years) was spent alone, doing my "job" while Tim was doing his "job" and my children were doing their "jobs." In hindsight, if I had my family life to do over again, this is where I would make the biggest change. I would train my children to participate in our family as a team. We would do most of our "jobs" *together.* We would make meals and clean up *together.* We would clean our rooms *together.* We would do yard work *together,* do projects *together,* and plan vacations *together.*

I encourage couples to work on their finances and their careers *together*. While they may go to work in different locations, they can support each other by sharing their business struggles and successes while gaining their lovers perspectives and feedback. In an environment of *Love* and safety, we can receive advice and constructive feedback from a perspective of *Love* rather than attack. We can listen with an openness to receive, rather than from a place of fear, with walls of protection built around us that keep us from hearing a valuable perspective.

One of the things I appreciate about my relationship with Joe is that we are creating our business together. I never feel like I am on the outside looking in. Joe respects my perspective, and I respect his perspective; after all, we are a gift for each other in so many ways. I want, and invite, his feedback on my work. I feel clearer making decisions having his male perspective to counter my female perspective. I feel part of something bigger than I could do on my own, and I feel more connected doing it *with* my lover even though I am fiercely independent.

As a life coach, I have learned that I can support my clients in their business goals without knowing one thing about their industry just by listening carefully and asking questions that open up new insights. This is true for our lovers as well, but we often miss this opportunity because we have a judgment that they don't understand what it is we do at work. Therefore, we lose the fullness of the gift that is right next to us every morning and evening. When we miss the many ways our lovers are a gift for us, we also miss an opportunity for them to feel as valuable in our lives as they could and to participate in life with us in more powerful ways. When we invite them to participate in as many ways as they would like to, we find ourselves feeling more connected, more supported, and safer in the relationship. This kind of connection, gentlemen, often times leads to a woman wanting to give you more of herself through sexual intimacy.

Women who feel connected and supported are more open to sex. If your partner is a woman, and she seems shut down sexually, she may not feel desired, connected, or perhaps there is an unresolved offense. I have observed that when men invest more of their time and attention in their women, the women, in turn, want to please them.

MEN AND TRANSITION

For men, transitioning between work-mode and family-mode is about a 30-minute process. Men *need* to be left alone for a minimum of 30 minutes *after* they get home to transition from their work thoughts to being present with their families. The drive home doesn't count, ladies! Men actually need to change their clothes as a physical reflection of changing their state of mind from work to home. Many women start talking as soon as their man walks in the door. I know by all appearances it looks like your man is home, but he isn't fully there yet. Both of you will feel frustrated if you attempt to engage him in conversations or requests before he fully transitions. Kiss your man when he walks in the door and then leave him alone until he comes looking for you to connect; then he will be fully present, and both of you will feel supported and *Loved*.

My Friend, this transition time is similar to what a woman needs to go from all of her responsibilities to sexual intimacy. However, for her, it's about 30 minutes of relaxing on a couch, sharing her day with you, or in a tub with a glass of wine.

MAKING *LOVE* SPICY

Preface: I will treat this topic as reverently as possible and I will be as specific as necessary. This is a touchy subject for many men and women. In the context of this book's purpose, it's not appropriate for me to do a thorough teaching on sex. There are many resources which can support your sexual experience beyond what I am offering here. Again, what I am offering in this book are the CliffNotes of what I have learned that works well to produce *Real Passion Revolution* in relationships. Please be open to considering my perspective and hold your judgments until you have read through this section for both the men and the women.

Let me be clear about this point: I do not advocate a woman submitting to sex with her partner if he is abusive in any way. I do not advocate a woman submitting to sex with her partner if there are any unresolved offenses between her and her lover. I absolutely do not advocate a woman using sex as a form of manipulation or control to get what she wants. My Friend, do not have sex with your partner because you want to keep peace in the relationship. If there is an unresolved issue and you engage in sex out of obligation, you will be betraying yourself and will likely resent your lover.

I believe that sexual intimacy is a *Spiritual* joining of two souls. For me it is a holy act between two lovers not to be abused. Many times our sex drive isn't really about the act of sex. It is about intimacy and *Spirituality*. The deepest meaning of sex is about becoming *One* with another. Sex reflects our longing to be deeply connected with *Love*. I *Love* this perspective by Bruce Marshall, "…the young man who rings the bell at the brothel is unconsciously looking for *God*."

Dear Friend, if we continue doing what we have always done, we will continue experiencing what we've always experienced. What is required to turn around most relationships is a new perspective that will support the necessary healing of the wounds you have ignorantly inflicted on each other. Many couples in long relationships have some serious injuries to heal before they will be able to enjoy a beautiful, fulfilling sex life again. I am writing this book to give you the tools you need to heal yourself and, in turn, your relationship. I want you to know that your healing is not only possible, but it's also essential for you to be able to experience a *Real Passion Revolution*.

Gentlemen, when you desire your woman sexually, it causes a sense of security for her. She feels that you want *her*, you are turned on by *her*, and you choose *her*. This gives her a feeling of peace in the relationship. However, because she is diversely focused, she is constantly hearing voices in her head compelling her to get something else done and demanding her attention. When you take her by the arm, hand, or lower back, and gently guide her into your bedroom, you are removing her from all of that stimuli.

Most women tend to feel pulled in many different directions. A woman needs to be able to relax her mind first, and then her body, to be able to experience sex in a way that is deeply pleasurable for her. I have had many female clients tell me that it helps significantly to have a glass of wine or two before sex to be able to relax into the experience. That may or may not work for your lover, so you will need to ask her about that specifically.

Fellas, it's important that you set the conditions which will best support your romantic rendezvous. Joe will invite me to sit on the couch opposite from him and put my feet on his lap so he can give me a foot massage. He will ask me questions about my day, about any conversations I had with friends, or about what I'm learning from a book I'm reading. He shows a genuine interest in what's going on in my world, in my mind, and in my heart, and that makes me feel connected, known, and *Loved* by him. Joe massages my feet because I told him how much I enjoy having my feet massaged and how relaxing it is for me. When I feel his loving care and attention, my heart opens up like a flower to the warmth of the sun, and *then*, I can't wait to engage in *Love*-making with him.

Light candles, make your lover a fragrant bath, pour her a glass of wine or tea, put on beautiful music (I recommend Lisa Gerrard or Hammock), make sure there is a lock on your bedroom door if you have children, even if they are asleep. It is a woman's worst nightmare to have one of her children walk in when she is naked with her legs in the air. Have that happen once, and she may never want sex again!

Remind her that you want to give her some pleasure amidst her chaotic day. If it's possible, it will support her greatly if you would offer to do one or more of the things on her list for making this time to pause for intimacy. If there are dirty dishes in the sink and laundry in the washer, she isn't going to want to get up after an enjoyable evening of passion and tend to those tasks. Make sex about meeting a *need* she has to feel connected to you. Relax her body with an intimate massage. Remind her that her body seduces you and turns you on. Then your woman will feel connected and be able to relax and focus on *Love*-making rather than on her endless list of duties.

When a man shows his lover he desires her, it nurtures the seductress in her. It reminds her that she is, above everything else, a woman. Being a mother, daughter, sister, or friend are all important to a woman. But being feminine, soft, and sensual is the core of most women, and we can easily lose touch with that part of ourselves in the minutia of the busyness of life. Making *Love* grounds us in our femininity and our sense of security.

Example:

Tim was so fearful that I would reject his sexual advances, or that I would have sex with him out of obligation, he wouldn't ask me for sex, nor would he indicate he even wanted sex, unless I initiated it. That couldn't have been a worse set up for me! As you can imagine, I never got to feel desired by Tim. I felt like he was doing me a favor by having sex with me. It didn't matter how many times I tried to explain my need to feel desired by him, or that I enjoyed sex and would never turn him away; he couldn't get past his own *story* to hear *me*. I suffered for many years because of this disconnection between us. I'm sharing this story with you, My Friend, because I want you to understand how significant it is that you make your lover feel desired, beautiful, wanted, and needed by you.

Men have a very different physiological *need* for sex than do women. While most women would never deny their lover food, they don't think twice about saying no to their lover's sexual appetite. It can cause a man physical pain to go without regular ejaculations, especially men between the ages of 16 – 45 or later, depending on their level of testosterone and stimulation, which is responsible for the production of sperm and semen. By the way, research shows a link between regular ejaculations and a lower rate of prostate cancer.

All of the beautiful, attractive things we women are drawn to in a man are due to the same hormonal response that causes them to *need* sex—testosterone. It's quite unfair to want our lovers to be strong, driven, adventurous, competitive, assertive, and masculine, but not horny. Until of course, it fits into our schedule, or they have performed in a way that we are willing to *reward* them with sex. Most women have a fraction of this hormone, compared to men, so our libidos are naturally lower.

As a woman, I would not be able to speak authoritatively regarding this significant difference in our sex drives except for the fact that, because of my total hysterectomy in 2004, I have been using testosterone cream to maintain a natural hormone balance. There have been times when I have mistakenly taken too much testosterone cream, and the impact has been significant. Not just a *desire* for sex, but a drive, a compulsion, a real *need* to have an orgasm—like gorging on food when you're starving because you haven't eaten all day. The few times I have had that experience, I've thought to myself, "This must be what it's like to be a man! Crap! How frustrating!" I also noticed that when my testosterone levels were too high, I literally couldn't get sex off my mind. I recall feeling like I didn't need romance or connection, just a quick release and then I could get my mind back to my day. But, until then, it seemed I couldn't shake that drive for an orgasm. It was embedded in my mind and my whole body. The simple solution for me was to be careful with my testosterone dosage; a man doesn't have that option, My Friend.

Women who judge men for being "animals" or "insensitive pigs" for *needing* a sexual release might do well to overdose themselves on testosterone cream and see where their perspective shifts. I'm sure I will get a lot of emails from men asking where they can get ahold of testosterone cream to put on their ladies while they sleep. It requires a prescription, gentlemen; so talk to your family doctor. The bottom line is this: we must realize that, physiologically, women are not designed like men. Our needs are equally significant *and* dramatically different.

Study after study shows that most men stray from their relationships because they were *starving,* in a sense, sexually and emotionally. Women often don't understand what is going on physiologically for men. For some reason, we have been taught that men aren't as sensitive as women, and they don't *need* to feel as deeply connected as women do, which couldn't be further from the truth. Many of them don't need to feel as connected as women do to *have* sex. But men feel deeply connected and vulnerable with their lovers within the context of sex. Women feel that same connection and vulnerability within the context of conversations in which they feel known and supported.

Strongly consider this, My Friend: What if your man rarely wanted to talk to you or spend time alone with you? How *Loved*, supported, or connected to him would you feel? Your girlfriends can help you meet your need for that type of intimacy at some level. But, what's a man to do? If his way of feeling *Loved* and connected is *through* sex, how is he to get this need met if you are unwilling to have sex with him when he is in need?

Do you have any idea how challenging it is for a man to ask for your help? In a sense, he is asking *you* for something he needs from *you* and with *you*. In a man's world, to "need" anything is a sign of weakness. When your man asks you for sex and you repeatedly deny his request, you have rejected *him*. Essentially, you have denied him *Love* and support. If you say "no" often, he's going to quit asking, and he will be left to figure out how to get his needs meet another way.

Pornography can be a huge problem in many relationships. Since men *need* to have orgasms rather frequently and their female lovers aren't as available as they *need* them to be, an alternative to sex (before or instead of infidelity) is masturbation to pornography. I have spoken to several men about pornography, and most of them would prefer to have intercourse with their partner than masturbate to pornography, unless there is a breakdown in the relationship in which case they would rather masturbate than have sex with their partner. Women, being ignorant about why men *need* so much sex, unknowingly set their lovers up for either masturbation to pornography, masturbation to his own mental fantasies, or to infidelity. Some women don't care if their lover masturbates to pornography. Some women are happy to be left alone. But, I assert that women feel this way because there is a breakdown in the relationship that has driven a wedge between them. Sex is an intimate, vulnerable act. No one is interested in being vulnerable with someone they don't trust.

Many men find themselves sneaking around to get some relief, which often leads to shame, not because masturbation is wrong, but because, either their female partner takes it out of context, or because our culture/religion makes masturbation bad. Shame, Dear One, has a huge ripple effect in our lives. It can lead to many unwanted and unhealthy behaviors including addictions.

At the very least, pornography is considered a big evil in much of our society. But men are visual beings, best sexually stimulated by what they see with their eyes. So, what's a man to do if his lover is neglecting his sexual *needs*? Is it possible the women in men's lives are inadvertently supporting the behavior they fear the most? Everyone has their own judgments on pornography. For some it is offensive for others, it's just a tool. Personally, I prefer my lover get all his sexual *needs* met by me, so I make it a priority in my relationship with Joe to "feed" my man when he's "hungry."

Joe and a close friend were having a discussion about the distinction between having sex and *Love*-making. They both agreed that there is an incredible level of emotional connection and a profound degree of trust involved with *Love*-making. Joe said that I am the first woman he has been intimate with where he actually felt like he was "making *Love*" to a woman. Not because he didn't *Love* other women—he deeply *Loved* his ex-wife of 20 years—rather, because he feels completely safe with me, and he wants to express his *Love* for me by *giving* me as much pleasure as he can.

I think Joe is responding to the freedom to be himself without any judgments, criticism, complaining, blaming, nagging, or his belief that he isn't enough. I believe this is the fruit of engaging in this intimate relationship in all the ways I have been teaching you in this book.

Again, My Friend, I am not bragging. I didn't make this stuff up. I merely applied all of the valuable tools and perspectives my mentors have taught me. It appears I have connected the dots of these tools uniquely as I have never heard anyone use them in the ways I've presented in this book. I notice the profound impact these tools have had on my happiness, on Joe, and on the quality of our relationship—and I want you to have this experience too.

Ladies, as I stated earlier, men need to have a "win" at home with their lovers. Since many men are highly sexual beings this "win" is very significant in the bedroom. If your lover just doesn't do it for you, then I suggest you *Lovingly* teach him what it is that you need to make *Love*-making more significant and pleasurable for you. Remember, My Friend, a man's greatest desire in an intimate relationship is to make his lover happy. Most men are more than eager to learn to be better lovers because their ego is so wrapped up in being successful in the bedroom. So, if need be, have a supportive conversation with him about spicing up your *Love*-making. I have spoken to many men about their sexual experiences, and all of them have said that what turns them on the most while making *Love* is giving their lovers intense pleasure. Sweetheart, don't hesitate to show your lover your own personal roadmap to an orgasm.

A word to the men: I know of some men who prefer their women not use any external stimuli during sex, like a vibrator. For some reason, these men feel less-than if their lovers can't have an orgasm with just their touch. Who is that about? Men have no idea of what it's like to be a woman when it comes to orgasms. 75% of women are unable to reach an orgasm during intercourse without the external stimulation of their clitoris. It would be like expecting a man to have an orgasm by only stimulating his balls. If your goal is to give your lover an experience she will want over and over again, then set your ego aside and do exactly what she asks you to do—not what you *think* she needs to climax. A woman's orgasm is about her, and every woman is different. Let your woman tell you, or show you, what she needs if you really want her to get the most out of your sexual intimacy.

Ladies, your man *wants you!* He *needs you!* He *chose you* to be his lover; you and I both know how significant that is to a woman! So enjoy giving your man pleasure and enjoy being his object of desire. Besides, sex feels good regardless if a woman has an orgasm or not, is tired or not, is horny or not. It is still physically pleasurable for both parties, especially if you allow yourself to be fully present with your lover. At the very least, if you're tired ladies, all you have to do is lay on your back and receive the pleasure your man wants to give you; he doesn't mind doing all the work sometimes. It's really not that hard to give a man a "win" in bed! Not to mention a "quickie" takes no more than 8 – 10 minutes for a man. Having said that, I don't recommend this as your usual *Love*-making efforts. It's just an alternative when a woman is tired or otherwise distracted and her lover is *starving*.

I invite you to drop your judgments about sex. Don't get caught up in the trap of thinking that sex needs to look a certain way or else it's cheap or he's just using you. He isn't using you; he's legitimately horny by no fault of his own. Your man doesn't choose to be horny any more than he chooses his heart to beat or his lungs to breathe.

Example:

I have a wise client Lisa, whose husband has a high *need* for sex even in his middle age and after being married for 25 years. Lisa learned many years ago that her husband's high libido was purely physiological, so she decided to work *with* his design rather than resist him and make life difficult for both of them. They successfully negotiated a sex-for-release schedule that worked for both of them, which was separate from their passionate *Love*-making. It's important to negotiate what we need or desire with our lovers. Many times we need to reach some compromise, but sometimes we can get all of our needs met simply by making a request—sharing what we need and being truthful about how we are feeling, without blame. Most people in a loving relationship are more than happy to try to meet each other's needs. If there are unresolved issues in your relationship, there will likely be a withdrawal from sexual intimacy. Addressing those problems, either within yourself via the *Holy Healing* process, with your lover, or with a relationship coach [me] will be necessary to create a clearing to be able to fully give yourself to your lover sexually.

While most men want to have sex for physiological reasons initially, once they have had an orgasm and the tension in their body is released, their brains are flooded with "feel good" endorphins and their hearts are flooded with gratitude for their lover. This is why men want to have sex after a particularly stressful day. It isn't unusual for a man to do and say the most beautiful, loving things after sex…just before he falls into a deep sleep. Your lover getting sleepy after an orgasm is also a response to brain chemistry; this is not him being insensitive or selfish.

Wanna drive your man crazy in bed? Wanna make sure it's *you* he can't wait to be with? Sure you do! Respect him a bunch! Affirm him frequently! Never try to control him! And give him a tantric massage. This is a method of massage for bringing your man to the edge of climax, then stopping the stimuli and massaging another area of his body. (It's called edging. Google it.) I recommend this approach for one of your extended romantic *Love*-making sessions as this technique would frustrate a man who just *needs* a quick release. The right music is an essential element for this kind of massage as it will provide both a rhythm for the massage as well as help you and your lover stay fully present with the experience. I recommend Lisa Gerrard or Hammock for your *tantric* listening pleasure.

My Friend, we are all way too busy! We have bought into the culture of "more is better." More stuff requires more time and more money, which requires more work. Busyness is a distraction *off* of our disappointments about our life, as well as a hindrance to our *Spiritual/*emotional growth. But, it is also a distraction *off* of what we claim are the most important relationships in our lives—our lovers and our families. "More" is *not* better; it's actually less! Less time, less connection, less intimacy, less energy! "More" robs us of those things that make life rich, rewarding, and most meaningful. Sacred writings teach us that *God's* ways are not man's ways. I am convinced that having more is simply man's attempt to be happy, but it's just a big black hole that sucks the life out of us. *God's* path to happiness is stillness, being aware of *God's Loving* presence and purpose in our lives, generosity, service to one another, *Loving* people, and finding our value in our true identity rather than in things.

Ladies, if you are too tired to give the beautiful gift of your body to your lover, then you need to take some things off your plate. Your relationship with your lover needs to be your top priority, so move things around, reassess your responsibilities, and find time to meet your lover's needs. If that just seems impossible for you to do, I suggest you ask yourself this question: "If there were a million dollars waiting for me at the end of this day if I reduced my responsibilities by one hour to spend with my lover, could I make the necessary adjustments to my schedule and activities?" Money is a great motivator of mankind—but it just might also be a light of truth that your relationship *is* or *is not* as valuable as money. Something to consider!

Which do you think your children would prefer, their sports and after school activities, or their parents having a strong relationship? Which do you prefer, more success in your career, or a passionate relationship with your partner? Sexual intimacy for both men and women is a huge part of a committed romantic relationship. It is impossible for me to cover everything about intimacy in this section, but it is also critical that neither partner minimizes this aspect of romantic *Love*. If you are not having a passionate *Love* life with your partner, you are missing out on one of the most beautiful, enriching experiences of being a woman or a man. I strongly recommend both partners read, *Loving Sex: The Book of Joy and Passion* by renowned sex therapist and expert, Laura Berman. It is both enriching and erotic to read this material to each other, which will likely get both of you turned on and off to a fun night of play.

Most of us have many friends but only one lover. The biggest distinction between the two is our sexual intimacy with our lover. It is sad and unfortunate to neglect fulfilling sexual intimacy with our lover and allow the relationship to deteriorate from one of passionate-playmates to one of friendship alone. I have had both situations so I can tell you from experience that romantic *Love* is a critical, underestimated part of a *Real Passion Revolution*. Keep sex alive in as many creative ways as possible. Not only does this facet of our relationship have emotional value, but it also has many health benefits for both men and women. My grandparents had sex into their 80s, and my grandma was proud to tell me! Trust me, you will be happier, healthier men and women for keeping this beautiful, vibrant, fulfilling part of your relationship a priority.

Dear Friends if you are struggling in your relationship regarding sex, remember that events are neutral; we choose the interpretation. It is the *interpretation* of the event which determines our state of mind and our emotional state. Our state of mind and emotional state is reflected in our energy and, ultimately, our peace and happiness, or fear and frustration! Sex is neutral. Choose an interpretation that best supports a *Real Passion Revolution* in your relationship with your lover.

Ladies, if you want your lover to feel supported by you and to desire you (which I know you do) then stop making sex for a man what it is for you; it isn't. If you want your lover to have a sense of wellbeing and to be able to focus on his responsibilities without the sexual distractions of either pornography or infidelity, then "feed" him when he is hungry! Stop resisting the way *God* designed men and support them with all of the tools I have given you here in this section.

When I told one of my male clients that *respect* (a man's greatest need) was equal to *desire* (a woman's greatest need), he was shocked that desire is so important for a woman! "How is that even possible?" he asked. It just is! The *why* is insignificant! Women could just as easily ask a man how it's possible he *needs* so much sex when women don't. It just is!

One could argue with and resist all of these differences, but at the end of the day, our reality will remain the same. It just is! I strongly recommend getting very comfortable with the *Law of Non-resistance*, taught by Raymond Holliwell in *Working With The Law*; it's been quite empowering in my own life.

My Friend, I taught you in the first section that the *pure purpose* in an intimate relationship is to *give—to Love*! "*Love*" is a verb; it is an action. *Love* is a behavior that is in the best interest of the object of our *Love*; our lover, our partner, our companion, our spouse. *Love* each other well, and *Love* will return to you in abundance!

It's time to change, My Friend! It's time to be healed and to be whole. It's time for a *Real Passion Revolution* in our world, and it starts with you!

*SECRET INGREDIENT 8 CONCEPT: *Understanding Our Innate Gender-differences*

1. Men's needs
2. Women's needs
3. Sex

FAN THE FLAME

1. What are the top needs of a man? Which 3 do you need to work on the most?

2. What is a man's greatest need? How have you failed to meet this need in the past? What can you do now that you understand this need?

3. What is a man's greatest fear? How have you facilitated this fear in the past? What can you do now to support your man to quiet his fear?

4. What are the top needs of a woman? Which 3 do you need to work on the most?

5. What is a woman's greatest need? How have you failed to meet this need in the past? What can you do now that you understand this need?

6. What is a woman's greatest fear? How have you facilitated this fear in the past? What can you do now to support your woman to quiet this fear?

7. Is there a breakdown in your sexual intimacy? What's working, and what's not working?

8. How can you best meet your lover's sexual need?

Dear God of All— In All, Thank You for the beautiful gift of variety within our genders. Open my eyes to observe, rather than judge, that which I do not fully understand. I now relax my mind into the awareness that men and women are created equal but uniquely different with specific needs. It is my deep desire to create a fulfilling relationship with my lover through understanding, compassion, grace, and love.

And so it is, My Friend, and so it is!

SECRET INGREDIENT 9

SPICY PERSONALITIES

"You know me inside and out, you know every bone in my body; You know exactly how I was made, bit by bit, how I was sculpted from nothing into something."
Psalms 139:15 MSG

We are all beautiful expressions of *Love*! However, we are quite unique in our natural approaches to life besides our gender differences. We have each come into this world with a particular personality type. There are many personality profiles we could learn from, but here I will recommend the two which have had the biggest impact on my relationships. If you are interested, I strongly recommend you study these two resources in depth.

I'm sure most, if not all of us, are aware that there are *born-introverts* (people who get their energy being alone) and *born-extroverts* (people who get their energy being with people). But did you know there are *born-Perfectionists, born-Nurturers, born-Achievers, born-Romantics, born-Observers, born-Questioners, born-Adventurers, born-Asserters, and born-Peacemakers*? These are the nine different personalities taught in the spiritual teaching called *The Enneagram.*

The Enneagram is believed to be the oldest (around 1200 – 1300 a.d.) and only *Spiritual* tradition of personality profiles. While I can't go into the many details of this teaching here, I can refer you to Fr. Richard Rohr who has been expounding on this material since the 1970s when he was introduced to it after he became a friar of the Franciscan order. Fr. Richard Rohr is an excellent, entertaining, and humble teacher. You can find his material at www.cac.org. You can also gain some understanding from an online site where you can take an online test to help you determine your own *Enneagram type;* www.enneagramworldwide.com

Here is an example which will help you understand how theses automatic dispositions may cause conflict in relationships unless we know what's really going on: When Joe was introduced to *The Enneagram*, he laughed out loud and said, "Oh my gosh, honey, there are other people just like me out there!" Up until this point, Joe thought he was the only person who processed life the way he did and gravitated towards fun like a kid. Joe is a 7, *An Adventurer*, on *The Enneagram.* He is motivated and compelled by pleasure, adventures, travel, learning, and freedom. One of Joe's close friends calls him, "The Mayor of Funville." Joe is the eternal Peter Pan, who revisits Neverland on a regular basis. These people *Love* the color orange and want their ashes to be spread all over Disneyland when they die. Joes favorite color has been orange for most of his life, and we just renewed our season pass to Disneyland.

People who don't understand that Joe's disposition and propensies are innate, rather than chosen on a conscious level, might have a tendency to judge him as being too playful and perhaps irresponsible. Depending on your own personality profile, you will either be drawn to a person like

Joe, or repelled by his sunshine. Joe has a friend, Michael, who is an 8 *An Asserter* on *The Enneagram*. This personality is the most opposite to the 7. Michael thinks Joe is crazy to be so happy and for committing to make fun a daily priority. He perceives Joe as being irresponsible simply because Joe is so happy and unburdened. After all, anyone who is *that* happy must not be carrying his weight in this world. Why is Michael worried and frustrated with Joe's disposition? Because an 8 actually gets energy from struggles and adversity, not from fun. They feel like they are making progress and are more alive if they are suffering and pushing through difficult challenges. The interesting thing is, Joe has had, at the very least, equal overall success as his friend Michael. And Joe has had a ton of fun on his journey towards all of his accomplishments.

I share this story with you, My Friend, because I want to give you a glimpse into the way our personality differences are perceived as bad, wrong, or dangerous, by those who don't otherwise understand that while we are all created equal, we are also very different.

My Friend, there are many more approaches to life than yours. Your approach and perspective is only *one* way, not *THE* way. The more open you are to accepting this concept the less resistance you will have with those who are different than you. The less you are resistant to those who are different than you, the more you can accept them with gratitude and even enjoy the variety of personalities in your life. Suffering is the fruit of resistance. Therefore, *accepting* bears the fruit of peace, joy, and freedom.

Problems arise in relationships when we think our way is the best, the safest, the most responsible, the most fun, the most powerful, etc., and therefore the least problematic. After all, I believe what drives us to want to control others or conform them into *our* image comes from a place of wanting what we perceive is in their best interest. But, if we lack understanding of how each of us is uniquely and intentionally made, we miss that all is well just as it is. With more knowledge we can relax into the mystery of all of the varieties of human beings, cultures, races, religions, and traditions.

The second and easier personality profile I have learned, and have used the most in my relationships and coaching practice is called, *In Living Color,* taught by my dear friend Daniele Hage. Daniele is the same mentor who teaches the class on men, *The Extraordinary Value of A Man (EVM)*. Again, you can find her teaching schedule at www. dynamictraits.com.

In Living Color states there are 4 personality distinctions, each represented by a color; *Reds, Blues, Yellows, and Greens.* There are other personality profiles defined by 4 colors as well, which might be slightly different than *In Living Color,* but the traits are quite similar. The reason I mentally access this profile most often is that it was the first human behavior profile I was exposed to, and it is super simple. In most cases, I am able to assess people (even strangers) into one or two of these colors simply by observing the way they dress, the colors they have on, and especially their energy.

The beauty and power I find in understanding human behavior, to the limited extent that I do, is that I am able to *speak their language* if you will. In many ways I get *them,* and that makes them feel known and understood. I would never expect a *Blue* to open up quickly and tell me their secrets. I would expect a *Blue* to be a loyal friend (once I've been thoroughly checked out). I would never expect a *Blue* to make a quick decision on most matters, so I would give them plenty of time to do some research before making a commitment to do something or purchase something. *Blues* have a tendency to have a first-response to a request as, "No." This *no* really means, "Give me time to think about it." If you preface a request to a *Blue* with, "I don't need an answer right now, I just wanted you to consider this…," the *Blue* will feel more peaceful about making a decision.

Remember I told you I have learned not to take anything personally from *The Four Agreements* by Don Miguel Ruiz? Understanding our personality differences is very helpful in doing just that. A *Blue's* hesitation to an invitation or request isn't about me; it's about the process through which a *Blue* is predisposed to making choices in their lives. It's not right or wrong; it just is!

A *Yellow,* on the other hand, says "Yes" to most anything that sounds like fun. These people want to know: who's going to be there, what are the activities, and can I escape if I'm not having fun? They will likely change their minds and cancel a prior commitment for something that sounds like *more* fun. Again, I would never take this personally since I understand a *Yellow's* propensity to follow the "Yellow brick road" to Funville!

Example:

One day, a dear *Yellow* friend of mine was feeling low energy (very rare for a *Yellow*). We had plans to attend a city celebration where there was going to be a large crowd of people attending. My then *Blue* husband, Tim, was dreading the crowds but willing to go for a limited time. *Yellows* and *Blues* are opposites in the colors profile. What I found to be enlightening and entertaining while watching these two opposite personalities was that the closer we got to the event, the more energy my *Yellow* friend displayed. By the time we saw the crowd of people, my *Yellow* friend was actually dancing in her seat and singing to all of us. My *Blue* husband, on the other hand, became quieter, while a sense of rallying himself for the challenge of being with so many unpredictable people overcame him. I watched him plan his route of escape, which included asking me how long we would be staying. These distinctions made me smile at both of them, and I became clear that we are not the same regarding what makes us feel happy or content. I observed how we process external and internal stimuli differently and need our particular preferred conditions to feel that all is well with the world.

Reds and *Greens* are also opposites. A *Red* enjoys a good debate/conflict and often challenges others to be equally passionate about their beliefs. *Reds* feel more alive when they get to compete either verbally or physically with their peers. *Greens,* on the other hand, avoid all conflict; they are peace-at-all-costs people. A conflict will shut down a *Green* and make them feel unsafe, whereas a conflict will cause a *Red* to feel closer and more secure with someone who can go toe to toe with them without being offended.

My oldest son, Jonathan, and I both have *Red* as our secondary color. We enjoyed having passionate conversations with each other, and neither of us felt uncomfortable during or after our friendly "debate." My *Blue/Green* husband felt it was his duty to stop this perceived "conflict" between his wife and his son, which made Jonathan and I chuckle at how much Tim's peace was disturbed by a conversation he wasn't even part of.

I hope you are beginning to see these differences. I encourage you to do more study to become competent at understanding the various personality traits to best support your lover and everyone in your life. Suffice it to say, if you can learn to leave space for the people in your life to be on their own journey, with their own unique personalities and preferences, you will discover more peace and happiness for yourself and for those around you.

*SECRET INGREDIENT 9 CONCEPT: *Unique Personalities*

1. Enneagram Profile
2. Colors Profile

FAN THE FLAME

1. Go to www.enneagramworldwide.com take the profile test and browse around the site.

2. Which number are you? Which number is your lover?

3. How are you different from you lover? How are you similar to your lover?

4. Check out this site for a color profile: https://www.colorcode.com/personality_test/ take the free online test. This is not my friends Color Profile, but it is similar.

5. Which color are you? Which color is your lover?

6. What new insights do you have as a result of becoming familiar with personality types?

Dear God of All— In All, truly You are a God of endless expression. How brilliant of You to have created each of us with so much variety and mystery. When we are fully awake and fully present life is quite the adventure and it is impossible to feel bored. Teach me to discover the brilliance and beauty in each complex personality. I desire to accept and appreciate everyone regardless of their innate personality disposition or the path they have chosen. My eyes are now open to observe others rather than make assumptions and judge them.

And so it is, My Friend, and so it is!

SECRET INGREDIENT 10

SPICY *LOVE*

"So I give you a new command: Love each other deeply and fully. Remember the ways that I have Loved you, and demonstrate your Love for others in those same ways."
John 13:34 Voice

Let me remind you of my definition of *Love*: *Love* is a behavior in the best interest of everyone including yourself. *Love* is an action verb; it is a behavior, not an emotion. We feel the emotions of joy, peace, and a sense of freedom when we are truly *Loving* or are being truly *Loved;* however, there is a catch!

Before I discovered the book, *The 5 Love Languages* by Gary Chapman, I couldn't understand why I didn't *feel Loved* by Tim. I knew in my head that he *Loved* me, but I didn't experience the warm *feeling* of being deeply *Loved*. Have you ever had this experience, My Friend? There is a distinction between being *Loved by* someone and *feeling Loved*. Or perhaps you genuinely *Love* your partner, but he/she regularly makes comments that they don't *feel Loved* by you; that can be so frustrating for both partners.

The 5 Love Languages brings new insight and clarity into this dilemma. Gary Chapman teaches that there are 5 ways in which people give and receive *Love*. We come into this world fluent in one or two of these languages of *Love* as preferences, but we can learn to recognize and appreciate them all. The 5 Love Languages are 1. *Physical Touch* 2. *Words of Affirmation* 3. *Quality Time* 4. *Acts of Service* and 5. *Gift Giving*. I want you to notice that all of these expressions of *Love* are actions; again, *Love* is a behavior in the best interest of the object of our affection.

Our fluent languages of *Love* have natural receptors, which pick up the signals of behaviors that represent our concept of what *Love* looks like. At the same time, we don't have the ability to receive those languages of *Love,* which are unfamiliar to us or that we are unaware of.

It's kind of like orange cars. How many orange vehicles do you see on the road? When I ask this question to my clients, the answer is universally, "None!" or "Hardly any." But, Joe and I see them everywhere. We actually see them all day long as we travel in our RV or driving around town in our car. Why do we see orange cars and most other people don't? Because we are *aware* of them; now you are too, and you will see them from now on as well. Just like orange cars, if we aren't aware that there are other languages of *Love* outside of the way we give and receive *Love,* we won't be able to recognize *Love* in those particular forms.

My primary expression of *Love* is touch; I touch people! I hug everyone I can, including any stranger who will let me. I rub Joe's head and shoulders, and I *Love* to hold his hand. If I'm close enough to reach someone during a conversation, I will frequently touch their arm, or shoulder, or leg as I'm making a point or while they are having an emotional experience. If I feel insecure or unsafe in a relationship with someone, I will be hesitant to touch them for fear of being hurt or rejected. For me, touch is extremely personal and vulnerable in any form; it represents *Love* to me!

My second expression of *Love* is time, which makes perfect sense to me because of my desire to connect deeply with people. I create intimacy with Joe, my friends, and with my clients by giving them the full attention of my time. I also enjoy blessing people by serving them. I will happily spend my time and my talents supporting you. If I notice you are struggling in any way, I will look for ways to lighten your load with practical help. I enjoy helping people! I will make you food if you are sick. I'll organize your home/kitchen/office/garage if you mention that you just don't have time to get through the chaos. I will pick you up or drop you off if you need a ride somewhere. Again, spending time with people or doing something *for* someone isn't just an activity; it's the way I show people that I *Love* them.

In my marriage to Tim, I often felt lonely and unknown. Tim's primary expression of *Love* was giving gifts, with serving others a close second. But Tim was also an Achiever (3) on the Enneagram, so the primary way he showed his *Love* for me was by working hard, long hours and buying me gifts. Since my primary expressions of *Love* are touch and time, and Tim was rarely around, I didn't *feel* very *Loved* at all, even though he really did "*Love*" me from his perspective.

I had no clue how starved I was for physical touch until, one Sunday morning, while sitting next to Tim in church and holding his hand, I was suddenly aware that for one hour each week, I was being touched by Tim. I *Loved* that *feeling* so much, and I cherished that time together in church. Tim didn't need touch; he didn't miss touching me because it didn't hold any significance for him. Since touch didn't hold any value for Tim, he simply couldn't understand why I needed it so much.

Example:

A perfect example of how we can miss expressing or experiencing *Love* with our partner in a way that is most meaningful to them is a Christmas *story* that I experienced in 2006, the year my son Jonathan served his first tour of duty in Iraq. On November 25th, the day I was hosting my family for Thanksgiving dinner, we received a call from Jonathan at 5 a.m. He was calling from the hospital after his military truck was blown up by an IED bomb. I won't go into all the details of this day or the event, but suffice it to say, as Jonathan's mother, I was a mess. Combine that experience with that holiday season being the first without Jonathan home; it made for a solemn Thanksgiving and Christmas season for me. What I longed for from Tim was his presence; I genuinely needed him to be close to me, to wrap his arms around me and hold me, to sit with me and help me get through this season of fear and separation from our precious first-born child. I needed Tim's touch and time, which I asked for over and over, often with tears streaming down my face. Unfortunately, Tim was unable to give me what I needed. I'm sure Tim's own fears and dealing with my pain was too overwhelming for him to be around. Tim wanted me to know that he *Loved* me in the only language he could communicate. During the entire month of December, Tim spent his work-free time shopping for special gifts that he thought would make me happy. Of course he did! He wanted me to feel his *Love* for me in the gifts I would open on Christmas Day.

Knowing Tim's expression of *Love* at that time, I was able to receive his gifts on Christmas Day with much gratitude and *Love*, but that Christmas season remains, to this day, the loneliest and the saddest holiday of my adult life. The gifts did not make me *feel Loved* even though in my head I knew they came from a place of *Love*. Tim totally missed what I needed from him the most because his expressions of *Love* were different than mine, and he couldn't imagine how comforting and healing his touch and his presence would be for me. In Tim's paradigm he couldn't have expressed his *Love* for me more, or blessed me more, than with those special gifts he found.

What I want to remind you of here is that *Love* is a behavior in the best interest of *everyone*. Can you see how Tim's choices met his needs but not mine? I'm sure Tim intended to meet my needs with his choices, but he only met his needs. He never actually listened to me or considered that what I was asking for. If he did, it would have had a significant impact on me. Had Tim set aside his perspective and preferred expression of *Love* and spent time with me or given me the gift of his touch, both of us would have had our needs met. Tim was *trying* to show me his *Love* it just wasn't in a way (language) that mattered to me.

What I found so beautiful about Gary Chapman's concepts was that once I began to recognize all 5 *Love Languages* and began *speaking* them for the sake of reaching others, I became fluent in all 5 of them.

Do you see, My Friend, how important it is that we learn to be fluent in all 5 *Love Languages* so we are able to say, "I *Love* you" in the most impactful ways to our lovers and anyone else who we profess to *Love*? If we merely observe the way people profess their *Love* for us, we will instantly know their particular expressions of *Love*, which will then equip us to support our relationships in a more beautiful fulfilling way.

Contrast my relationship with Tim with my relationship with Joe. Joe's primary expression of *Love* is also touch, second is time, followed by service. Like me, gift giving is barely on Joe's radar. Since our expressions of *Love* are the same, it is both easy and natural to fill each other's *Love*-banks up throughout the day. If Joe is close enough to touch me, his hand is resting on me or gently caressing some part of my body. At the beginning of our relationship, Joe's constant touch was so shocking! I would literally take a deep breath and feel overwhelmed that he enjoyed touching me without me asking that of him. I *feel* so *Loved* by Joe every single day, and I don't think I will ever get used to his tender *Loving* touch; he still takes my breath away!

CONCLUSION

I recognize it might seem conflicting to teach you about minding your own business, doing your own healing work, and reframing your lover as a gift, especially when your partner pushes your *buttons,* and then to teach you how to navigate within a relationship full of inborn differences to reduce the risk of conflicts. So, which is it? Whose *business* is our differences? If my *buttons* get pushed by some ignorance on my partner's part, like my need to feel desired, whose responsibility is it to address, mine or my partners? The simple answer is, it is *always your* business, and to *your* advantage, for *your* happiness, to do the work of healing *your triggers* and to obtain the knowledge to best support *yourself* and your relationships. It is never your business to tell your partner to address his buttons or to gain knowledge about your differences. The best way to teach your partner is by demonstration. Joe has picked up all of my tools by being with me not because I told him he needed to change.

I felt the need to share these differences between our genders, personality profiles, and expressions of *Love* simply to make it easier for you to best support your relationships through understanding. I discovered that once I understood all of these inherent differences, I was able to engage with others without resistance and cause less frustration for myself and everyone in my life.

While Joe may support me feeling desired and secure in our relationship through his knowledge of a woman's needs, I still need to do the work of addressing all of my insecurities and frustrations whenever they arise. Knowing and implementing supportive behaviors with each other eliminates resistance to that which we do not understand and adds another level of joy, fulfillment, and ease to our relationships, but this does not heal us.

Tim didn't embrace the journey I was on. He didn't do the work of his own healing or gain an understanding of our differences; I did. The result was that I felt empowered and healthier, year after year, which had a dramatic impact on *my* own happiness as well as on our relationship. I was able to stay in our relationship without causing myself or him more pain. Tim suffered the majority of his short life considerably. Sacred writing teaches that *God's* children are ruined because they don't know what is right or true; they don't understand *God* or *His* ways – *Hosea 4:6*. Tim passed away at 55 years young in 2014 from a massive heart attack. He is sorely missed by many people who deeply *Loved* him but could not heal him.

I use *all* of this knowledge in *all* of my relationships. I'm sure you have heard the saying, "Be the change you want to see in the world." Or the Golden Rule, "Do to others what you would have them do for you." I want to be *Loved*, whole, understood, and accepted for who I am without having to conform into the image of someone else. This is what I am *giving* in my relationship with Joe and everyone I'm in relationship with; it is what I am living out daily for you, Dear One.

I want to emphasis this, My Friend: When I say, "I *Love* you," if *Love* is a behavior, an action verb, rather than a feeling, and, if the object of my *Love* is you, then doesn't it make sense that all of my choices would be in consideration of what is in *your and my* best interest, including those actions/choices which communicate to you the clearest and loudest that you matter in my life and that I am here for you?

What many people really mean when they say, "I *Love* you," is, "I feel happy with you." This *feeling* we call "*Love*" is actually joy. "I love my car" is, in reality, "I feel happy driving my car." "I love pizza," would be better said, "Eating pizza gives me pleasure."

In the same way we misuse the word "*Love*" for inanimate objects, we also misuse the word "*Love*" regarding people; this is why we can be so confused when someone says they *Love* us but then treat us unkindly; the words and *actions* don't match.

In this context, there were many times in my relationship with Tim that he wasn't making choices in *either* of our best interests; therefore, not loving me in actuality. Rather, he *felt* joy being around me, and he believed he needed me to be happy. I recall one conversation I was having with Tim when he was insisting on his *Love* for me. I realized that it might be more accurate to say, "I *need* you very much" rather than, "I *Love* you very much." It became apparent to me that Tim's actions were less congruent with *Loving me* and more aligned with *needing* me. I do believe Tim was doing the very best he could with what he understood at that time. I believe the same applies to you and me, My Friend, as well as for your lover. What is powerful to recognize is that simply "doing our best" doesn't always have the best results. We need to be conscious enough to *examine the results* of our choices to see if they are working or not working to produce the experiences we want for ourselves as well as for the other people in our lives.

Eckhart Tolle teaches in *The Power of Now,* "*You cannot Love your partner one moment and attack him/her the next. True Love has no opposite. If your "Love" has an opposite then it is not Love but a strong ego-need for a more complete and deeper sense of self, a need the other person temporarily meets."* I assert that if your "*Love*" has an opposite, then you are trying to *get* something from your partner that only you can give to yourself. The *"more complete and deeper sense of self"* is the healing which takes place by addressing your *emotional buttons* and reinterpreting your childhood *stories* with *Love* and *truth* through the *Holy Healing* process. Personal wholeness (complete, lacking nothing) is what makes us experience healthy, healed, happy relationships.

The impact of deeply understanding your lover is profound! Joe and I have had this discussion several times. *Love* begets *Love*! *Love* wins, but only 100 percent of the time! The more I praise and respect Joe, the happier he is, and the better he does in life. The more I do to support him, the more he wants to make me happy. I observe Joe doing things *just to make me happy* because *he* feels so *Loved* by me. The crazy thing is, the more Joe does to bless me, the more I want to do for him. We are each responding *to Love with Love*. Hindu's call this the cycle of karma. Christians call this process of sowing and reaping. This is The Golden Rule: *"Do unto others as you would have them do unto you."*

Love without an agenda, and *Love* will return to you in full!

*SECRET INGREDIENT 10 CONCEPT: *Understanding Different Love Languages*

1. Expressions of *Love*:
2. Touch
3. Affirmation
4. Service
5. Time
6. Gifts

FAN THE FLAME

1. In what ways do you show *Love* to others?

2. In what ways does your partner show you he/she you?

3. Do you *feel Loved* by your partner?

4. Does your partner *feel Loved* by you? (Ask them what it is you do that they feel *Loved* by you)

5. Regarding these expressions of *Love*, what do you long for most with your lover?

6. Do you know what he/she longs for most with you?

7. In what ways does this knowledge support your relationship with your lover?

8. What shifts are you making as a result of this new information?

Dear God of All— In All, Thank You for all of the variety and mystery of Your creation. I am a student of Your revelations and perspectives. Align my understanding with Yours. Teach me to rest within the mysteries of life knowing that You are my Teacher, my Guide, and the Great Love of my life! You, Dear God, are The Way, The Truth, and The Life within me and without.

And so it is, My Friend, and so it is!

THE RESULTS

"Love endures with patience and serenity, Love is kind and thoughtful, and is not jealous or envious; Love does not brag and is not proud or arrogant. It is not rude; it is not self-seeking, it is not provoked [nor overly sensitive and easily angered]; it does not take into account a wrong endured. It does not rejoice at injustice, but rejoices with the truth [when right and truth prevail]. Love bears all things [regardless of what comes], believes all things [looking for the best in each one], hopes all things [remaining steadfast during difficult times], endures all things [without weakening]. Love never fails [it never fades nor ends]."
1 Cor. 13:4-8 AMP

Gaining new and significant, even brilliant, insight is not transformational; daily application of that new insight or revelation is what will transform your wounded *Spirit* and fear-driven-mind, and, in turn, transform your life.

Do the work, My Friend! Become a healed healer for your lover and for everyone you *Love*, for we can only take others as far as we have gone ourselves.

My deepest desire for you, My Friend, is a *Real Passion Revolution* of your own! I believe what I have shared with you here has more power than even I understand. I believe this is the cure for failed and failing relationships. This approach to healing, health, and happiness is not a quick fix. It is challenging to face our fears, to change our automatic thought process, to release control, to drop our judgments, to challenge our perceptions, and to interrupt our *stories*. With enough practice and persistence, you can transform your mind, transform your relationships, and transform your state of happiness. This is what I believe Jesus spoke of when he said, "Truly I say to you that unless a man be born again he cannot *see* the kingdom of heaven." The Kingdom of *Heaven is* here, now, within, and available at all times. Most people are blind to the Kingdom life because they are allowing their fearful thoughts to be absolute truth rather than challenging those thoughts and allowing *Spirit* to give them the perspective of *Love*. Jesus is referring to us having *Spiritual* sight to re-*new* our minds—to correct our thoughts and our behaviors so we can *see* what has always been true: the Kingdom of *Heaven* is right here, right now! When we tune into *Spirit,* we heal our minds and enter the Kingdom of *Heaven* where only *Love* exists, *Love* abounds, *Love* directs, and *Love* wins!

I encourage you to read this book often to stay grounded in these concepts. Work through the exercises every time you suffer, feel stuck, are fearful, want to control someone, or want to abandon your own business to be in someone else's business. I take myself through all four steps of *Holy Healing* every time my peace is disturbed, and my peace is restored without fail. I don't know if there will ever be a day when *all* of my buttons are *fully* healed, and my peace is *entirely* undisturbed. What I can tell you is that as a result of having done this work and implementing all of these tools, my peace is *rarely* disturbed. Whenever my peace *is* disturbed, it is for moments now rather than for hours or days and it is never, no never, about Joe! As you continue to do this transformational work, you will gain momentum and watch your state of happiness evolve to levels you have never imagined possible. Now, go, fan the flame!

Dear God of All— In All, What a wild adventure! Truly, Your perspective and Your approach to Love and life are so very different than man's best efforts. Teach me all of Your ways that I might Love well and bring healing and happiness to my life and through my life.

Love **Well My Friend— Welcome To the Revolution!**
Denise Darlene TLC
Transformational Love Coach

For personal coaching support, contact me at:
www.denisedarlene.com

MENTORS & RESOURCES

BYRON KATIE byronkatie.com

WILL BOWEN willbowen.com

DR. WILLIAM GLASSER wglasser.com

RAYMOND HOLLIWELL [Working With The Law available on amazon.com]

DANIELE HAGE dynamictraits.com

ECKHART TOLLE eckharttolle.com

GARRY CHAPMAN 5lovelanguages.com

DON MIGUEL RUIZ [The Four Agreements] miguelruiz.com

FATHER THOMAS KEATING contemplativeoutreach.org

RICHARD ROHR [Enneagram teaching] cac.org

ENNEAGRAM INSTUTITE enneagraminstitute.com

COLOR PERSONALITY CODE colorcode.com [similar to Daniele Hage's class]

DR. LAURA BERMAN [Loving Sex: The Book of Joy and Passion] drlauraberman.com

Personalized Powerful
Individual & Group
Coaching

"I just completed 6 coaching sessions with Denise Darlene that were truly transformational and powerful. She has a unique gift of lovingly and authentically opening the channels of vulnerability and to expand one's heart to search diligently into the deep recesses of the soul and spirit to find treasures of possibility and destiny. Utilizing the highly effective techniques and revolutionary ingredients of her profound book "Real Passion Revolution", a whole new world of contentment was unveiled as years of repressed fear and pain were discovered and brought to the surface to be healed and introduced to a fresh perspective of love and forgiveness. With the inspiration and help from Denise, the future now includes a world where the best possible version of myself has blossomed and the fragrance of hope, peace, love, and purpose can emanate generously upon others so that the newfound freedom I have experienced can be shared, taught, granted, displayed, illuminated and become available to all."
Scott Parsons - January 28, 2017

More info at denisedarlene.com/work-with-me

reInvent

reInvent is a 10 week online course that dives deeper using one concept a week. These concepts are pulled directly from this book Real Passion Revolution. Joe & I have recorded live events that teach these concepts with humor and compassion. After you sign up you'll be given access to video content that makes learning these concepts easy and fun to discuss and implement with your partner. When applied, these concepts will transform your relationship from broken to beautiful. They are essential if you are in a new relationship, as these tools will safe-guard you from the most common destructive behaviors nearly all couples engage in. Read this book first and do the exercises at the end of each chapter. You'll be on solid ground. If you desire to go even deeper, ReInvent is your next step. Sign up before May 15th, 2017 for only $79. That's 60% off.

"Having read numerous iconic self help books and having been a student of scripture and timeless teachings all my life, I admittedly began reading Real Passion Revolution with a skeptic's heart. What I discovered in the pages of Denise's book was truly enjoyable, challenging, and unexpected! It's as if the reader has the opportunity to sit at the feet of their beloved family matriarch or community Pastoral figure and experience teachings on love, acceptance, and self reflection directly from an inspired source. The stories and examples that are weaved throughout the pages are equally as entertaining as they are profound. To say that this book is making a difference in the lives my partner and I would be a major understatement. I know of no single other source of teaching and inspiration that has made a bigger impact on our relationship and growth together. I'm happy to say that this skeptic has become a true Real Passion Revolution believer!" - Aaron Ball / CEO and Founder of Ballpoint Communications Group(Florida)

Sign up at denisedarlene.com/work-with-me

reNew
Transformational Love Course

This full-day, intensive, experiential workshop will introduce you to a radically new approach to relationships. You will learn powerful new relationship tools that support rather than undermine your relationships. The tools I teach will help you uncover the hidden fears that govern your life and are wrecking havoc on your relationship. You will learn how to get your needs met in a real and profound way that lets your lover off the hook. You will learn how to engage with your lover in a way that protects the relationship and prevents the most common wounds most couples ignorantly inflict on their partners.

More info at denisedarlene.com/work-with-me

Made in the USA
San Bernardino, CA
15 March 2017